The Diary of a Northern Moon

GLORIA WALDRON HUKLE

Bloomington, IN   Milton Keynes, UK

AuthorHouse™
1663 Liberty Drive, Suite 200
Bloomington, IN 47403
www.authorhouse.com
Phone: 1-800-839-8640

First published by AuthorHouse 9/20/2007

ISBN: 978-1-4343-2675-1 (sc)
ISBN: 978-1-4343-2674-4 (hc)

Printed in the United States of America
Bloomington, Indiana

This book is printed on acid-free paper.

IN LOVING MEMORY

OF

Bertha Yvonne La Croix

1908–1983

Remembrance

Remembering, fondly, Carol Waldron Thomas;
her devotion to Waldron genealogy is not forgotten.

TWELVE GENERATIONS AGO

WALDRONS APPROACHED NORTH AMERICAN
SHORES.

THEY SETTLED IN NEW NETHERLAND.

THREE HUNDRED FIFTY YEARS LATER

IT SEEMED

ALL TRACE OF THEM HAD DISAPPEARED.

Waldron Family Crest

At the time of William the Conqueror

(Circa 1066 – 1087)

PREFACE

The town of Johnsburg, New York, is located in the northwestern part of Warren County, approximately sixty miles north of the state's capital city, Albany. The communities scattered throughout Warren County are a part of the magnificent Adirondack Mountain Region. At the base of Gore Mountain lies the tiny hamlet of North Creek and at the edge of the town, behind the Baptist Church (formerly the Free Will Baptist Church), the Union Cemetery. It is here amid the old stone markers that this story, as well as my first novel, MANHATTAN: SEEDS OF THE BIG APPLE, was conceived.

It's quiet up there on that hillside. With the exception of a lone bagpiper who shows up on occasion, the only sounds that one might hear are the faint whispers of souls pleading recognition. Even though each tablet bearing family names such as Waldron, Roblee, or Freebern represents the alpha and omega of one unique journey, I was drawn toward two slabs in particular.

Midway through the 18th century Waldrons joined with Knickerbockers, Quackenbos, and Bradts, to become a part of the colonization of a large fertile tract of land purchased from the Mohawk Indians by the City of Albany. This early settlement, later called Schaghticoke, is between the Hoosick and Hudson River Valleys of Upstate New York and, although rich farmland, was meant to be a buffer zone for Albany, New York. (Similarly, a century earlier, the village of New Harlem had provided a protective shield from hostiles for the city of New Amsterdam on Manhattan Island, scene of MANHATTAN: SEEDS OF THE BIG APPLE, and home to the first of the Holland-born Waldrons to settle on these shores, Resolved Waldron.) It was here at Schaghticoke, in the place that history would call "The Vale of Peace", and in the Dutch church established by their forefathers, that William Waldron, 5th generation descendent of Resolved, and eighteen year old Judah Bradt married in 1804.

Sometime around 1816 the Waldrons and their six children left Schaghticoke and traveled northward, settling at Elm Hill, a mile south of Johnsburg. They were among the first settlers in the area New Yorkers traditionally refer to as the "North Country". Will and Judah and their children remained at their Elm Hill log house for a few years before moving to the village of North Creek. Eventually the family would comprise fourteen children.

Many of us experience several "new beginnings" in our lives. Just as Will's and Judah's cemetery markers were a new beginning for my quest to discover more about my ancestors, so Elm Hill was a new beginning for hundreds of people in their quest for a brighter future in the late 18th Century.

Word had spread about the opportunities held within the hidden wooded slopes of northern New York. In 1797, before

Americans thought about tagging a slice of social history with terms such as Industrial Revolution, Elm Hill founding father, John Thurman, put up a cotton factory. Soon, along with the help of an innovative group of new English immigrants, his print mill factory began producing calico cloth (believed to be one of the first in America). Logging and pot ash mining and manufacturing (used for soap, glass, and ceramics production) also thrived, as did the grist mill and a distillery.

Throughout the years, because of my unquenchable thirst for early New York history as well as personal ancestry, I continued to learn about these Adirondack Waldrons and their ancestors as well as many of the families who touched their lives. Adirondack pioneering during the first half of the 19th Century and that relentless, can-do American spirit were parts of the anatomy of all brave enough to settle the then wilds of upper New York State. Their fortitude has been passed down to the scores of offspring generated from those original inhabitants. Ground breakers all, North Country people were trailblazers long before the California Gold Rush drew many of their cousins west.

* * * *

A fictionalized, dream-like journey inspired by Will and Judah Waldron and several more recent family members, THE DIARY OF A NORTHERN MOON, like all such narratives, holds a good dose of truth.

In 1976, for Tena Waldron, a young advertising executive, all of the aforesaid history was lost somewhere among the long unopened pages of her grandmother's family bible, disco bars, and too many leisure suited men.

Blank pages are about to be filled when a gift of change and antiquity wrapped in brown paper is delivered to her apartment.

Discovering her fatherland, discovering this fatherland, was long overdue.

INTRODUCTION

"This is the building," Kay announced, double-checking the address written on a small piece of notepaper pulled from her jacket pocket. The tall brunette paid the cab driver seventy-five cents, and the yellow taxi vanished around the corner.

Kay glanced warily at the petite woman standing beside her in front of the four-story brownstone housing the City Morgue, her slight frame rigid, her brown pumps seemingly frozen to one small slab of sidewalk. Observing her mother's frayed, brown tweed coat, Kay felt her heart jerk as thoughts went to her kid sister, Tena, who waited with their Aunt for her and her mother to return. Of course, Tena was too small to understand the shock of this morning's news, but, one day she would ask questions and when she did, Kay wondered what her mother would say. What could any of them say about Tena's father? Who really knew Ben Waldron?

Staring blankly at the grey band of pigeons that had anchored themselves across the ledge of the stone transom above the building's main entrance, Kay tried to remember when it was that her mother had said she last heard from

Ben? It seemed as though that must have been just before Easter last year. *Could it have been a year? Could it really have been a whole year that he was gone?* She returned her attention toward her shivering mother. "Ma, are you okay? It's cold and clammy out here. Maybe we should go in?"

Quietly Bertha Waldron responded. "I don't think I can do it, Kay."

"Sure you can. But, if you think that you would rather not, then I'll do it. One of us will have to identify the body. We have to be sure that it's Ben. Who knows, maybe there is some mistake."

"Try to understand, Kay. I don't have to see his body to know he's gone. I know it's him. I feel it in my soul."

Kay took a deep breath. The dampness of this awful March day had gone straight through to her soul as well. "I want to help you."

"Yes, I know, dear. I do appreciate your support."

"I think that you'll probably have to fill out paperwork and show some sort of formal identification," Kay said, softening her voice. She was feeling increasingly ashamed of her bitter thoughts about Ben. She said, "They always want something as proof, don't they?"

Bertha responded, "Yes, documentation. There is always that. I suppose I have to pull myself together. After all, it isn't as if this is the first time I've been through this sort of thing, and I know God is good. He will see me through it all again. Don't worry, I'll be all right."

Kay nodded.

Clutching the dark brown straps of her vinyl handbag, Bertha fought to regain her composure, whispering, "I went into the strong box before you picked me up at the house. I think that I have everything that I'll need."

Kay whispered back, unsure of what should be said or left unsaid. "What about Ben's brother? Should you try to reach him?"

Exhausted, Bertha sighed. "Let's just get this over with."

The two linked arms and walked up the steep, cold, slate steps leading to the Morgue's glass double entrance doors. Once inside, each pulled the other forward, sure that if either one let go their task would never be accomplished. As they approached the reception clerk, Kay stepped assertively in front of her mother. "We've come to identify the body of my stepfather."

"Name of the deceased?" the woman asked without looking up from the pile of papers spread out next to her Underwood.

Bertha nudged Kay to her side. "Ben Waldron," she answered nervously.

"And your name?"

"I'm Bertha Waldron. I'm his wife." She handed several documents to the clerk who Kay thought offered a rather pasty, lifeless smile of consolation.

"Wait here, I'll only be a minute," the woman instructed, disappearing behind the polished oak railings.

Bertha dabbed her eyes with an embroidered white handkerchief. Obviously feeling faint, she steadied herself against the deserted oak desk and observed her daughter dismally. "I suppose you think that I'm crazy. You probably think I'm nuts to cry over him after what he put all of us through."

"I don't think you're crazy, Ma."

"I just wish…" Bertha stammered. "If only I had known. I might have been able to be with him in the end. Oh, dear Lord, how I wish he had continued with the AA program."

"I know, Ma. Try not to cry. You know, I just thought of something else. What about Ben's first wife? Didn't he have a son by her?"

"I never knew much about her."

Kay sighed. "I'm so stupid. I shouldn't have asked that."

"It's all right, Kay. I know this is very hard for you too. All I can say is that Ben told me that she remarried, and the little boy was adopted by the new husband. Oh God, I know I should have stayed with him. Maybe I could have saved him."

"You had to leave for Tena's sake. Let's face it; he was his own worst enemy."

"That's true, Kay, but he couldn't help himself," Bertha replied tersely. "God forgive me, but I wasn't strong enough. What's worse is that nobody was able to help him. Naturally, I'll contact his brother. They used to be very close, you know."

"No, I didn't know that. How would I? Do you have his address?"

Bertha seemed oblivious to Kay's bland sarcasm. "I have it someplace, but I haven't heard from him in nearly seven years, and, of course, he's never seen Tena. He's still out in Idaho with his family as far as I know. And, there's his Aunt Mary living over in Troy. Of course, I'll do my best to notify them as soon as possible."

Kay didn't reply. She had never met any of Ben's relatives, and she really didn't give a hoot about Ben's brother. He hadn't bothered to come to the wedding in '49. He had ignored her baby sister. She was sorry that she had mentioned him, yet she found herself thinking about something Ben told them one evening over a game of pinochle. He talked about how his brother had left New York State and headed out West after the War. If she remembered right, his brother had purchased land out there with the money he had sent home while serving in the military. It seemed that after the war Ben's brother had been involved in a government program building prefab bungalows to house discharged servicemen and their families. Building houses piece-meal seemed like a wacky idea to her, but Ben said that his brother sold quite a few of them, and he made good money doing it. Right now Kay couldn't even remember the brother's name, but promised herself that as soon as today's ordeal was done with, and her mind was clear, she'd do what she could to help her mother locate him, because where on God's earth would her mother find the money for a funeral? Her mother cleared barely forty dollars a week at the factory. She and Jake could help out a little, but…

Her thoughts were interrupted by the return of the receptionist and a lanky, young man in a light gray suit. The receptionist gave them a quick glance and went back to her desk. The man smiled and extended his hand. "Mrs. Waldron?"

"Yes."

"I'm Nick Brian, the Assistant Coroner."

Bertha politely acknowledged his introduction. "This is my daughter, Kay LaMarsh. Would it be possible for her to make the identification?"

Mr. Brian moved toward Kay, once again extending his hand. "I'm sorry we meet under such circumstances. It is legal for you to identify the body if you are twenty-one. Are you?"

Kay nodded her affirmation.

"Follow me then, but we require your mother's presence in the room along with you." He held open the spindled gate.

As they walked through the corridor, Bertha was suddenly overwhelmed with the need to give an accounting as to why she had not come sooner, saying, "The policeman said on the telephone that apparently my husband had a heart attack. He died during the night, but I wasn't called until only a few hours ago this afternoon, and then I waited for my daughter to come home from work." Bertha felt her face growing warm. "I suppose the police had a difficult time locating me because my husband and I were separated in 1954."

There was a moment of silence before Mr. Brian asked, "Any other children?"

"I have a little girl. Ben is her father. My sister is minding her now."

The young man observed Bertha curiously. "You were told of the circumstances of your husband's death?"

"I don't know what you mean? As I said, I was told it was a heart attack." Bertha replied, obviously confused.

Nick Brian stopped mid-stride. He leaned closer, putting one hand on Bertha's shoulder. "Ben Waldron passed away, I'm afraid, next door at the jail, and to be honest with you Mrs. Waldron, we're not quite sure if it was a heart attack or not. The police found him dead in his cell just after dawn. He had been brought in for drunk driving last night, and, of course, all of this is under investigation, but I was under the impression you knew. I'm sorry."

Feeling as if she had been slapped, Bertha replied softly, "No, nobody said anything like that to me."

"Well, there's a little more to it. You see, because the officer on duty and I are old friends, I was told something else about your husband's last hours. The officer said that Mr. Waldron had been sober enough to ask for a pencil and paper at approximately ten P.M. Later he asked for a glass of water, and Officer Russell brought it to him. From what I understand from the officer, other than the effects of too many drinks, your husband seemed fine. Everybody over there is pretty shaken up about this. Anyway, when your husband's body… that is, if the deceased is your husband; when he was found they looked into his wallet and saw that he had listed you, his wife, as next of kin. He carried a snapshot of your younger daughter, too. Well, look, understandably this is terribly hard for you. Let's just have you make the identification."

Both Kay and Bertha were visibly shaken as they continued to follow Mr. Brian to the end of the hallway where he opened the door to a small, sparsely furnished room. Bertha hesitated at the entrance, turning toward Kay, "I'm all right now, Hun. You should wait out here for me."

"No Ma, I said…"

"I know, but I owe him this much and after all, Kay, this isn't your responsibility. Now, don't worry."

Reluctantly, Kay stepped aside as the Assistant Coroner and Bertha walked into the room, closing the door behind them. Bertha approached the covered corpse with quick steps and stood silent. Mr. Brian lifted the sheet, never taking his eyes off the woman beside him. Her head pounded as she forced herself to look into the lifeless face of her husband. She made the sign of the cross. "It's him."

"You identify this man as your husband, Benjamin Waldron?"

"Yes, it's him." She turned away feeling herself weaken.

After replacing the sheet Nick Brian gently took her arm. "Come sit for a minute. You did just fine. Would you like for me to get you a cup of water from the hall fountain?

"No, I'm all right, thank you."

"We need you to go through Mr. Waldron's personal things," he said, nodding in the direction of a long table by the far wall of the room.

"Yes, of course."

"Eventually, you may take your husband's possessions along, but I'll require a signed acceptance."

"I don't understand. What do you mean by eventually?"

"Well, because your husband was found dead in the cell, there will be a delay of a day or two until the investigation into his death is concluded, and so these things won't be released to you until then. I hesitate to mention it now, but an autopsy might also be required before a final cause can be determined."

Bertha's mind whirled as she opened the metal box and began to remove one item at a time. Mr. Brian didn't move from her side.

"As you can see from his identification card he had a flat over on Clinton Avenue," he ventured quietly.

She lifted her head to speak, but no words were left, only thoughts. Bits and pieces of a life once sweet with tender intimacy floated in her head.

"Take all the time you need, Mrs. Waldron, I'll be just outside the door keeping your daughter company," he said, leaving her alone to examine what Ben had carried with him only yesterday.

Slowly she reexamined the identification card and a worn photo of Tena as a baby. Painfully she recalled how he had jokingly nicknamed her "his little pumpkin girl."

Behind the snapshot of their child she found a penciled note, obviously a draft letter to her. Tears streamed down her cheeks as she read.

Bert, you did right to leave me. I never wanted to hurt you. You and Tena mean the world to me. I know it's hard for you to believe in me anymore but an hour ago I promised God that I'm going to get myself straight. Times have been bad, Bert, but things are going to change. I swear it. I'll be in touch again when I'm presentable.

If you think of it, say one of your powerful prayers for me.

Love,
Your Big Lug,
Ben

Taking a deep breath, she reached into her purse again for her handkerchief, quickly pressing it to her eyes. Although he had been gone from her for what seemed a lifetime, she felt the despair of loneliness like she had never felt before.

After a few more moments of deep contemplation, she replaced everything into his billfold and then put it, along with his apartment key and a half of a pack of Camels, back into the container. Placing her husband's last possessions on the table she walked toward the exit sign, the fine blonde hairs on her arms standing up as she thought she heard faint lyrics to "Fascination."

As *their song* drifted through her memory, Bertha had only one thought –

Why did it have to end this way?

Chapter 1

1976 Upstate New York

Jack's Oyster House's black tie, all male waiters had been serving lunch through the usual conversational crescendo in competition with the ping-pang clang of glasses and plates for more than fifty years. This afternoon was no exception. The large paneled dining room of Albany's most trendy downtown restaurant pulsated with a familiar mix of politicians, manicured office workers, and briefcases.

"Here's to you, Tena." Cindy said, lifting her coffee cup. "Double congratulations are definitely in order."

Tena responded to the toast in accordance. "Thank you. I'm so glad we decided to meet here today."

"Yes, I am too. Did you see Mayor Corning? He just left."

Tena nodded, glancing around the room. "This place always brings back old times, doesn't it?"

On cue Cindy raised her cup again. "To those good old times and golden new ones as well....and, may we forget what was rotten."

"I always admire your can-do, staunch bravado, Cind."

"What can I say? It must be my Scandinavian blood."

Smiling back, Tena added, "Yes, of course, to the Vikings then and to the future."

Swallowing a last bite of apple pie, Cindy studied her friend, an acknowledged super ace in the advertising field, the demanding, razor-edged profession they mutually shared, and she marveled how anyone so accomplished professionally in this cut-throat business fell so easily into deadbeat relationships. Dressed in a tailored, sage-green suit, Tena's long, shiny red hair was pulled back into a French twist that exposed her flawless cameo complexion. She speculated that anyone who saw her would swear that Tena Waldron was at the top of her game. She put up a fantastic front.

Cindy said, "You're quiet today, my friend. You seem down. So when are you going to tell me what's really going on?"

"I'm not down; just thinking."

"You're thinking?"

"Well, thinking as a constructive mental process may not be an exact description of what's going on inside this head. It's a stretch for me to be constructive about anything these days, but, believe me, I am trying."

Cindy sighed. "I know you're trying. Don't be sucked into a place you just don't deserve. All things considered, that would be far too ridiculous."

"You're a good friend, Cind."

"Look, I suspect that this undercurrent of confused melancholy that's come over you has something to do with Ken? If you're down about Ken, don't be. He was never right for you, Tena."

"I'll console myself with that thought."

"That,' Cindy whispered leaning closer, "is the same line that you gave me when I was drowning with Billy Van der Heyden? Remember that jerk?"

"What do you mean?"

"You said we were two people in different orbits, and you were absolutely right. So be kind to yourself, and be kind to me, and get on with the festivities."

"That was different, and I never thought Billy was a jerk."

Cindy narrowed her eyes. "He was a jerk to me."

"You were never even close to drowning."

Cindy lit up a Cool, exhaling the smoke over Tena's head. "Listen, how many of us celebrate a birthday and win the city's prestigious Diamond Award all in the same week? Don't give me that 'nobody has suffered as I have suffered' attitude. Come on girl; you should be doing cartwheels! Your cake is sprinkled with diamond dust this year."

"You're right. Absolutely, a birthday should be a new start, or as my mother would suggest, *the opening page to a new chapter in life's book*. And, of course, I sure won't stick my nose up in the air at the five hundred dollars."

Cindy's eyes widened. "Five hundred! And here I was thinking how impressive the trophy would look on the coffee table in your new apartment."

Tena replied sheepishly, "Not that I pooh-pooh the trophy either. Really, it's great!"

"There you go. That's the winning spirit I like to see. You know, I think the Diamond Award might be a catalyst for good things to come. Don't you worry about what happened with Ken. This may sound weird, but I sense something fantastic is going to happen to you."

"But honestly, my head isn't as full of Ken as you seem to think. I really..."

Cindy cut in. "I'm not making this up just to make you feel better. I really have had you in my thoughts and always picture you surrounded by a bright light."

"Oh, God, Cind, not the bright light thing again."

"Well, it's all good stuff. It's an uplifting sort of feeling. I just can't explain it, only to say that it's a positive vibe."

Tena chuckled. "The truth is that you are a worse dreamer than I, Mrs. Maxwell, but I sure have reasons to be open to your positive thoughts this afternoon."

"Wonderful."

"You know, it's rather strange we're having this conversation because I've had the feeling that something is going to happen in my life. Up until recently, I thought that the change would have something to do with Ken, but you're right – that's a dead-end street."

"Thank God you've come to that conclusion."

"It's hard for me to explain. Anyway, I'm sorry I've been such a drag these past few weeks. Honestly, I do appreciate you listening to all my blubbering on the phone, but I swear to you that I've got my bearings again with my personal life. So, I want you to relax knowing I'm done with the one who has been the biggest jerk of all. Will you do that for me?"

Leaning back into her chair, Cindy answered cautiously. "I'm as limp as that giant lovely willow by Peck's Pond."

"Now, if you give me a chance I have something important that I want to talk to you about."

"What do you mean?" Cindy leaned forward. "I'm all ears."

"Good, because there is a story here, and I'll need your full attention. It appears that someone, and I have no idea who, wanted me to have an early birthday present."

"Really?"

"A couple of days ago my neighbor on the second floor, Jan Healy, called after I got home from work. She said that she had taken in a small package wrapped in brown paper that had been delivered to me, and so I went down to pick it up. Everybody in my building helps one another out this way."

"Good place."

"Yes, it is. Anyway, inside the little box, wrapped in white tissue paper, was a tiny silver spoon with the engraving, 'P. W., 3 May, 1725'. As I said, I have no clue as to who sent it. I don't know what the monogram means, either. There was no return address on the package or card attached."

"Wow! So, where was the package postmarked?"

"Warrensburg, New York."

"Interesting."

"Yes, more than interesting; wow is right! I showed the spoon to my mother. She thinks it looks like a funeral spoon. I guess my mother's Godmother, Lydia Beekman, had a few that were sort of family treasures. Hundreds of years ago the Dutch used to give these spoons to people who attended a funeral as a keepsake. She had no answer for the postmark. Nobody seems to know anyone in Warrensburg."

Cindy frowned. "I wish you had brought it along to show me. Who could 'P.W.' have been?"

"I don't know, but the only connection that I could possibly imagine is that he or she was a Waldron. I can't help but be fascinated with the journey this spoon had to make into my palm and why on God's good earth would anyone send it to me?"

"Very, very strange," Cindy mused.

Tena leaned against the back of her chair and winked. "I've planned an odyssey for myself, a way to open up the windows of time."

"Ah, drama. An odyssey sounds so intriguing."

"You'll be pleased to know that I have something I did bring with me, and I want to show it to you." Tena reached down alongside her seat into her briefcase. After scrambling for a few moments in her bag, she dropped a small, gold band into Cindy's hand. "My mother continued to wear my father's ring for years after he died. Before she married Otto she gave it to me."

"Such a tiny little thing."

Tena nodded in agreement. "Sure is. After the spoon arrived the other day, I found myself in one of those nostalgic moods and was rooting around in my jewelry box. I have some of my Grandmother's broaches that I was trying on with my new suit. I wore one the evening I accepted the Diamond Award.

"Anyway, I came upon my mother's ring. Foolishly, I tried it on my ring finger, and needless to say, it stuck. I panicked. It was a stupid thing to do because, of course, I know that my mother's ring size is smaller than mine. After tugging and soap I finally was able to get it off. I guess I took the episode as a sign that I should stick to my guns this time."

"Hold on, you're loosing me. What do you mean 'stick to your guns this time'?"

"Oh, a couple of years ago I was about to do some serious family-roots searching, and then you can guess what happened – Ken came into the picture, and that was that. But now, I feel, well, it's almost as if my father calls to me."

"Of course," Cindy interjected.

"I've decided I'm finally going to take the forbidden plunge."

"A forbidden plunge sounds ominous…and somewhat worrisome to me."

"Maybe *forbidden* is a bit strong, but my mother always either ignored or discouraged any conversations regarding my father. At least, that's how I've seen it."

"I know you well enough, Tena, to see that you're determined, and that you have something very specific in mind. I might want to talk you out of it."

"Wasn't it you who said that good things were coming my way?"

"Okay, keep talking."

"I've told you how my mother always makes such a mystery out of anything to do with our life with my father."

"Yes, you have."

"It's just that I know so little about him. I don't understand why my mother is so reluctant to talk about him. It's always been a source of confusion for me. She said she was in love with him when they married, and I do know that it was his drinking that split them up before he died. Of course, it's really hard to find out anything because his parents were dead when I was born, and as far as I know, he doesn't have a single surviving relative. And there is something else that bothers me."

"What's that?"

"It's not only my mother who is quiet about my father and that part of her life. My sister is also closed mouthed."

"Do you think that possibly it could be that Kay just doesn't have a whole lot of information to pass along to you?"

"Not a chance. What I think is that Kay and my mother made a pact long ago. They decided that some things, at least where I'm concerned, are better left unsaid. When it comes to any of us in the family, my sister is a bit of a she-wolf."

Cindy smiled. "Funny, I've always thought that my sister and yours have similar personalities. She-wolf is an interesting description, yet a tad bitchy don't you think?"

Tena continued unperturbed. "It will be a miracle if I find out anything, but I think it's the right time to unearth a miracle. I'm going to the Adirondacks and dig up all that I can about my dad. After all, I've passed through the birthday quarter."

"You sure are melodramatic today. I want to hear more on the dig, but what in the world is a birthday quarter?"

"I've turned twenty-six. You know, a quarter of a century has been filed away."

"How dreary."

"I guess the spoon pushed me over the edge"

"Oh, I get it now. And I want you to know that I won't waste my breath trying to talk you out of anything. In fact, I'm glad you're going. This is a slice of your life that you've set on the back burner for a long time."

"Well, thanks, Cind."

"When are you going? I know that this could turn out to be the adventure of a lifetime, but it could be a little scary too: walking into a maze of unknowns. Are you nervous?"

Tena shook her head assertively. "No, not really. I have scheduled vacation coming up, and I thought I'd use it constructively. To tell you the truth, originally I had very different plans for my time off from the Record, but, who knows, maybe this is destiny, especially considering that suddenly I have an extra five hundred available. I guess you're right – the award really gave me a kick start. I'm excited at the prospect of doing some genealogical detective work."

"Right on!"

Sipping the rest of her coffee, Tena said, "I'm just anxious to get away. You know what I mean. A roots search will keep me occupied while I try to heal up."

Cindy returned the ring. "That's a special piece of gold, and oh, what stories could be told if that little ring could talk. Besides which, you should see yourself. You light up just talking about this venture. Does your mother know you're going?"

"No. I haven't had the opportunity to sit and talk with her about much of anything lately. She doesn't know anything about what's happened between Ken and me either, but I'm headed over there tonight. Heaven only knows what I'll say about Ken, and I'm also worried what she will have to say about me going up north. Still, I've made up my mind."

"Absolutely, you have to talk all this over with her. Don't get me wrong, I still think that you should go, but you two need to talk."

"I know we do, but as I said before, it seems that anything having to do with that section of her life causes her to close up like a clam. I suspect it was a more difficult time for Mom than she lets on. You know, I don't want to stir up painful memories, yet I have this desire to know something about the man who gave me life."

"I can appreciate your dilemma. It's understandable that you wouldn't want to hurt your mother. What do you plan to do with that ring?"

"I'm going to have my birthstone set into it. When I suggested the idea, she was delighted. I'll wear it as a pinkie ring."

"Oh, Tena, that's a nice idea. And who knows, maybe giving you the ring represents closure to your mother, and now she'll be more open to your curiosity about your dad."

Tena shifted in her seat. "My only concern is my mother…"

"You don't have to explain. I know how close you two are. Any girl who goes to her mom's house for dinner once a week undoubtedly loves her mother. I've never believed that you craved pot-roast that much. Do you still go every Thursday?"

"Some things never change," Tena replied.

"My impression of your mother has always been that she cares very much about her daughters, and it follows that she will want you to do whatever it is to give yourself a sense of peace."

"I hope so."

"Well, maybe you'll do all of that and find Mr. Right in the process."

Tena stiffened. "I'm not interested in any more men."

Cindy looked at her watch. "But you will be," she sang out softly. She picked up the check.

"Say hi to Dave. You know Cind, they broke the mold with your David."

"You're right. I wish I didn't have to, but I've got to get going. I have an appointment over on Pearl Street."

"Thanks for listening."

"Thanks for sharing. When you're ready to have a serious nervous breakdown and leave the newspaper business, come over to the magazine aisle. We would be happy to have you on board at Today's Home."

"I appreciate that," Tena said, pushing back her chair.

When they were in the parking lot Cindy called over her shoulder, "I'll call you over the weekend. I'll be dying to hear how you made out."

Chapter 2

Tena winced as her right front tire grazed the edge of the stone curb in front of her mother and stepfather's house. Shutting off the ignition, she leaned back into her seat observing the six o'clock gyrations of her old neighborhood while listening to the loud, rhythmic blend of at least a half dozen lawnmowers at work, a customary Thursday evening routine. After a day at the paper it was refreshing to sit for awhile beside this ancient emerald splash. The expansive, lush carpets bordering Lansingburgh's worn centenarian slabs of gray slate were great-grandchildren of seeds planted generations ago. Naturally, they deserved respect. Watching the Bowen brothers toss a football back and forth in the middle of Grand Avenue, she wrestled with how she would open the conversation with her mother.

In front of the 1813, two-story, white frame residence that had been her home, her stepfather, Otto Pollock, struggled with a stubborn garden hose. Her eyes rested on the short, slightly round figure wearing brown-rimmed glasses and green coveralls. As if a snake not to be charmed, the hose fiercely resisted his efforts to be wrapped into neat sections to be put away this evening.

Rolling down the car window, she called out, "Hey, Ott, how you doing?"

The man introduced to her mother a dozen years before at a Parents Without Partners meeting acknowledged her arrival with a broad smile, clearly happy to see the youngest of his and Bertha's joint clan.

Tena waved back as she got out of the car and made a mental note to pick up an anniversary card.

"Your mother's been waiting for you, Tena," Otto called over the fence.

"Yes, I know. I'm sorry. I wanted to be here sooner, but I had ads to get in by deadline."

Otto nodded and went back to winding the last section of hose.

Passing though the unlatched swing gate, Tena wondered what Ott would think about her plans to rummage through the whispery gray areas of her childhood. She suspected her mother's reaction, but how would he react if he knew that his wife was dead-set against the venture? Tena had begun to question if she really had the right to open doors that had been kept tightly closed for decades.

"Hi, Precious,"Bertha greeted warmly while holding open the front screen door. "What were you doing out there so long?"

Pausing at the door, Tena pushed in two of her mother's dangling rhinestone hairpins that were about to fall from her upswept coiffure. She kissed her softly rouged cheek. "I was watching the guys throw a football. I see Buddy has lost his tantalizing long locks. What a shame."

Shrugging, Bertha said, "Like his dad, he had his heart set on the Marines. I guess we really can't think of Buddy as being one of the block kids anymore."

Tena wrinkled her nose. "I haven't thought of Buddy as a kid for a long time, but it's hard for me to think of him as a Marine either."

"I suppose," Bertha said with a sigh. "So you were just watching the boys? I was worried – it's after six."

"I don't know what's with me today. I had lunch with Cindy, and ever since I'm in slow mode. Then, I had ads to throw into the layout room, and afterwards I made a quick stop at my place. I picked up my mail. I was just flipping through it for a minute and saw that Kay sent a postcard from Florida. By, the way, Mom, Betty did a good job on your hair today."

"Oh, you think so?" Bertha felt the back of her head for the possibility of more renegade pins.

Tena suppressed a smile and walked toward the side bay window where she saw Otto closing the garden shed door. Over her shoulder she said, "Kay seems to be having a good time."

Bertha said, "Did she have anything interesting to say?"

"No, just having a great time. Come on anyway, how much can she say on a postcard?"

"That's very true."

"But, she did surprise me with a call for my birthday last night."

"Goodness, a card and a call. Your sister loves you dearly, that's for sure. I imagine she must have you on her mind and felt badly about not being here for your cake. I think it's the first time."

Tena followed the loosely tied sash of her mother's ruffled pink apron toward the kitchen. "Hi Peanuts, you conceited little thing," she whispered as she passed the parakeet's cage. Peanuts continued to peck wildly at his blue reflection in the miniature mirror. "I expect that you know that they put money down on a vacation house there. From Kay's description on the phone it sounds very nice. It's right on the beach."

Bertha opened the door of the GE, swinging out one of the refrigerator's glass shelves laden with dishes of food wrapped in wax paper. "No, I didn't hear a thing about it."

"Come on now. You knew all about this. Don't you try to kid me. Kay never gives me any news before you two have had ample time to thrash it over; you're stuck together like Elmer's glue."

"Oh, stop it. You always think that there is something going on that you don't know about."

"So you didn't know anything about the Florida place either?"

"No, I am just hearing it from you now. Cross my heart."

Tena observed her mother with an air of disbelief, but decided to let go of the possibility that another conspiracy between her sister and her mother had been hatched. "I don't know much more. Kay says she'll fill us in when they get home."

Bertha said, "Let's change the subject. How did your lunch with Cindy go this afternoon? How does she like married life?"

"Lunch was terrific, and by the glow she radiates, I'd say she likes her role as wife quite well. By the way, she said to say hello, and she wants me to bring you over to see their new house."

"Nice for her to invite me, I didn't know that they bought a house."

"Yes, they moved in last month. She was her perky self, and it's obvious she is content. She says she feels centered. I think David gives her balance."

"That's good to hear. Balanced is a good way to feel. I'm happy for her."

"You know, Mom, I felt good just being with her, but, of course, that's nothing new."

"Of all your friends,' Bertha reflected, 'Cindy is one of my favorites."

"About Kay, Mom, I know that Kay and Jake would love it if you and Ott went down to see their new place this winter. I think that they have family vacations in mind. That's probably why they're buying a big place."

"No, I don't think that we could go," Bertha responded slowly.

"Why not?"

Bertha began filling the saltshaker. "We can't go this year because we're going to Wisconsin to tour the cheese factories."

"That's right. I remember you talking about going." Tena sighed, suddenly feeling overwhelmed by the necessity to get to what was for her the point to this particular visit. "Mom, listen, I have something that I want to tell you about."

"Of course, I wouldn't want to hurt their feelings," Bertha mused.

"Speaking of vacations," Tena offered casually. "I'm thinking of going up north. Maybe I'll hit Lake George, or I might even get around to going up as far as North Creek. I thought that I'd like to check out where my father grew up."

"So you're still considering going up there? I know that you talked about it last year. I just can't understand what the attraction is for you," Bertha responded tightly.

"I have the time and a little extra money, and I've decided to go."

Bertha placed the green, carnival-glass butter dish on the table. "What more do you need to know? I've told you everything there is. The past is the past. It's gone, Tena. I would imagine that there isn't anyone left up there who would have known him."

"It's just something I need to do. My father's been dead for over twenty years, but he's resurrected inside of me, and I can tell you that lately he's been a very active ghost."

"Oh, Tena, don't carry on so."

"Yes, I know you think I'm being dramatic, but I need answers that you can't give to me. I have these dreams…"

"What dreams?"

"Just dreams. I don't think that you would understand. How could you understand when I don't understand?"

"Try me," Bertha persisted. "You always told me your dreams when you were a little girl. Remember when you thought you saw a tall man standing in your bedroom doorway?"

"Oh, my gosh, that was a long time ago, Mom."

"Yes, you were very small, and it was just you and I against the world in those days. But, I understood then. Maybe, if you give me a chance, I could understand now. You might be surprised; I wasn't born yesterday, you know. I've had my share of heartache and rough times and, God knows, bad dreams."

"Of course you have, but these are a different kind of dreams. To be honest, I'm afraid that you'll think I'm headed for the loony bin like Great Aunt Millie."

Bertha paused, obviously flustered. She studied her daughter. "I'll bet that all this has something to do with that spoon somebody sent. As for Millie, Tena, you have nothing in common with your Aunt's situation. God bless her. The poor woman couldn't face the insults that Louie continuously thrust upon her. It was a sin the way she was treated."

"All we can hope for is that Louie gets his, and that it's true that what goes around comes around. About the spoon – you have to admit a little spoon dated over two hundred years ago is an unusual gift, and stranger still, with no card attached. I'd say that's enough to stir up a mystery."

"This whole thing about the spoon makes me nervous, Tena. I don't like the idea that you received an anonymous gift. It just puts me on edge. Who would do such a thing? And I'll tell you what else, I'm nervous with you putting in all these late hours at work. It's just not safe for you to be coming home late at night by yourself. And then on top of it all, ridiculous that you put in all these extra hours and never get paid for it."

"I'm not alone, Mom. It's just different from how it was when you were working at the dress factory. We're all on salary at the paper. When you're on salary everybody works extra hours, and besides, I love my job."

"I still think that's nuts and seems worse than being on piece work. When we did the extra we expected to get paid for it. I'm glad you like your job, dear, but I can see too that you need to get away from it. I'm worried about you and so is Otto. You know he loves you as much as I do, and we see you preoccupied, losing weight, and we're concerned. I'll tell you something else: I'm never going to get used to you living all alone either."

"I suspect where this is headed. I should marry Ken, have a cart load of babies, and then I sure wouldn't be living alone."

Flatly, Bertha replied, "I've never said anything like that to you, Tena."

Tena reached for the paper napkins from the countertop, slapping one beside each of three of her mother's blue everyday plates already on the kitchen table. Her mother had no clue whatsoever about how deceitful some men could be today. She would never trust another male the way she had trusted Ken. If only her mother knew that Mr. Wonderful had announced to her on her birthday that he was interested in someone else. In fact, he had been seeing this other woman while dating her. His confession implied that he had even been sleeping with her. Rage was beginning to flow through her veins again.

Turning to her mother she said, "Mom, I wish you would stop worrying about me. I'm just fine in my little studio apartment. As for my weight, I deliberately dieted so I would look good in my bridesmaid gown for Cindy's wedding. I'm really pleased that I've been able to keep it off this long, and I'm perfectly safe with Mr. and Mrs. Walsh in the apartment just above me. In fact, I've made friends with just about all the people in my building."

"I know it's a nice place. I'm just concerned about you."

"I know, Mom."

"You know, Tena, you might try praying. God does help us get over the bumps."

Tena stiffened. "Please, no preaching. You know I believe He's up there, and I do pray, but I have come to believe that God helps good people like you who have the big faith more than apathetic believers like me who just muddle along. You have a direct link."

"Where did you ever get that idea? Are you trying to tell me that you're not a good person? I appreciate your loyalty, but I'm far from a perfect being. Still, as flawed as I am, I know He hears me when I pray. You need to give God a try, Tena."

"Okay, I'll try again, Tena replied weakly.

"Don't get discouraged. Everything will work out."

Tena studied her mother. *How did she ever come up with that kind of faith*, she thought. Softly she continued, "I often think of how fortunate I am to have had you for a mother. Don't think for one minute that I've forgotten all those nights you read to me when you were half asleep after pumping those sewing machine pedals at the factory all day long. You've always been there for me."

"Dear Lord, Tena. I'm your mother!"

Tena sighed. "It had to be so hard on you. I know that there were a lot of women who would have given up. You could have walked out, or just stuck me into St. Catherine's Home and walked away, but you didn't."

Bertha stared at her in horror. "Why would you say such a thing?"

"It's true, you could have."

"No, I could never have done that. I never gave orphanages a thought. As for those other children in foster care, maybe the poor mother had no other alternative. I was lucky: Grandma Honey, your sister and Jake were always there to help me."

Tena said, "I guess I'm not saying what I want to say very well. I love you, and I want you to understand that you are a wonderful mother, but your constant love and wisdom doesn't erase the fact that I still want to know about my father. Each parent gives their child twenty-three chromosomes; it's half and half, not one who hands out forty six."

Bertha sat down at the table and folded her hands. "You should be as persistent with your prayers," she murmured. "Of course, I understand that although I was a single parent for a good many years, I wasn't your only parent."

"I didn't mean to be disrespectful."

"You're not going to let this business go about your father. Are you?"

Tena smiled. "Just look at my stubborn role model. Mom, you've told me all you know, but it sure wasn't much. You don't know anything about his parents. You didn't even know how much money my father made when you married him. Don't get mad at me, but frankly, I'd never marry anyone who didn't disclose his income."

Bertha sighed. "I guess this is what they mean on TV when they talk about a generation gap. You won't believe this, but in those days people didn't impose themselves into another's personal business."

"What do you mean?"

"It wasn't a matter of secrecy; it was a matter of respect for privacy. So, I certainly wouldn't have considered the amount of your father's paycheck important when he proposed."

"All of the women in your day must have been blinded by love," Tena replied cynically.

"Oh, do you think that's such a terrible way to be?"

"Yes, as a matter of fact, I do."

Bertha chuckled. "The girls of your generation must go to sleep at night with dollar signs in their heads and awaken in the morning the same way."

Tena winced, "I don't know anyone that bad, Mom."

"Maybe I can explain how we were with a little story," Bertha began. "One day your Uncle Adam came home with your Aunt Ruth, and her boy, Peter, who at that time was only seven or eight. Adam introduced Ruth as his wife and that was that. Your grandmother and I didn't ask him any questions. Now, keep in mind that Adam was thirty-eight years old, and still lived at home, so bringing home Ruth with her child was a very big surprise because none of us had the slightest notion that he was regularly seeing someone. We were curious about Ruth, of course, but we respected their privacy and accepted her for the sweet woman that we came to know. Years later, your cousin Beth came along, and at a late time of life for Ruth, just the way it was with me when I became pregnant with you. Your Aunt and I were in the same boat. We became very close, but never once did I ask her a question about her past life. Whatever had happened was none of my concern, and if she chose to keep it to herself that was her business. She extended the same courtesy to me later on after I left your father. What I'm trying to say is that if someone wants to open up the private pages of their lives that's different. Otherwise, the book should stay closed."

Tena felt hope slipping away. "Are you saying that's what you think I'm doing with this trip north—prying into private pages? Do you think it's wrong for me to want to go to the town where my father grew up and possibly see the school and church that he attended?"

Wiping her hands on her apron Bertha mused, "I think that you should do what you feel is right."

The two looked up as the screen door squeaked open. Otto poked his head in. "I need to go up and wash. Give me another ten minutes."

"That's fine," Bertha called after him as she placed the roast onto the platter, covering it with foil. Turning toward Tena she thoughtfully continued, "Since I can see that you are determined to proceed, I suggest that you start your quest at the town hall at North Creek. As you know, both his folks were dead when we married, but I met two of his aunts, and there was an uncle, although I never met him. They should have the records there.

"I've met a few of his relations. I can tell you a little about them. They were wonderful, warm Christian people. Alma never married. She lived up north in a small town, Bakers Mills. She died when you were a baby. His Aunt Tess lived in Plainfield. I remember that she was a missionary. She spent some time in China, I think."

"China?"

"Well, Tena, the truth is that we were never close, and after your father died, we exchanged Christmas cards for a couple of years, and then we lost touch." Bertha lowered her voice to a near whisper, "I began to date a man. It wasn't anything serious, and nothing ever came of that, you understand. At that time I had no intention of remarrying, but I was lonely, and he was a nice fella. I didn't think that your father's family would understand my seeing someone. Now, looking back, I suppose that was silly, but it was how I felt about it at the time, so I never made a big attempt to keep in touch. I assume that by now if Tess were alive she would be past ninety years old."

"I don't remember you going out with anyone when I was a kid. What happened to the mystery man?"

"I don't know; we only went out a half dozen times, and Lord, that was so many years ago."

"Why on earth would they care if you dated someone after my dad was gone? But getting back to my father's family, I never remember hearing anything about his aunts."

Bertha answered indignantly. "I don't recall you asking about your father's people until recently."

"I was afraid to ask you about them."

"Why, for goodness' sake, would you be afraid to ask me anything?"

"Maybe because I thought that there was something terrible about him. Oh, I know he was a big drinker..."

"Yes, that was his downfall. The drink killed him."

"I don't know, Mom, I guess I just thought my dad and his family would be a taboo topic."

Bertha sighed. "I'm remembering how your father used to tell me about his ancestors. They were all Dutch people on his father's side. The Waldrons came from the time of early New York and Peter Stuyvesant. He said his family had been living in the Adirondacks for generations. He had quite a few crazy stories, come to think of it. He claimed that through one of his great-grandmothers he was part American Indian, but I think he was just teasing."

"Mom, I think Grandma Honey told me this tale."

Bertha laughed. "I'm amazed that your grandmother ever listened to a word Ben had to say. I'm sure she thought he was full of bologna. Your father could tell such a good story that I'd never know if it was a fairy tale or gospel. Well, I never did believe that he was part Indian. For certain he didn't look like an Indian. He had hair redder than yours, and such white skin. He fried in the sun, just like an egg in the pan, just the same way that you do."

"Really?"

"Oh, yes, and one time he had a terrible case of sun poisoning and ended up in the hospital. Did your grandmother ever tell you the one about the Dutchman who ran off with his brother's slave woman?"

"No, I've never heard that one."

"Supposedly it happened way, way, back, and it had to do with the first Waldron who came over from Holland. He had a couple of brothers that came over too. For the life of me, I can't remember any of the names, but I do remember the story somewhat. The one brother was killed, and his family taken prisoner by the Indians, but eventually they escaped and made it back to New York. The other surviving brother was a printer, and he fell in love with his brother's servant woman and ran off with her to the Ohio wilderness."

After a moment of silence she added, "I'm sure that I never told you, but it was your father who named you after one of those ancient Dutch relatives. I liked the name Kathleen, but he insisted you be called Tena."

Tena was captivated. "No, you never told me. I wonder who could have been Tena?"

"I don't know, but by the time you were born I was quite fond of your name. From the first time I looked into your sweet little face the name just seemed to suit you."

"Did you love my father as much as you loved Kay's?"

"Oh, Tena, I was very young when I married Henry. When he was killed I was lost. We had been childhood sweethearts, and after that happened, well, I felt as though I couldn't go on. But with the love of my family and God's help I did go on and found new love."

Tena felt her chest tighten. She looked at her mother sadly. "But loving my father only brought you more heartache. I know you left him because of his drinking."

"As far as your father and I were concerned, the end was painful, but, oh no, I don't look at our getting together like that," Bertha replied softy. "I was grateful that God gave me a second chance. We had many good times, and if I hadn't met your father, I wouldn't have had you. I would have missed a very special gift."

"You were very brave," Tena reflected.

"Not brave, just in love. I do understand your need to know more about your father, yet at the same time, as I said, I think you're wasting your time because I don't think anyone is left up there."

"The ground where he walked is still there, isn't it? Mom, something – someone – is telling me to go. Who knows, maybe it's the first Tena urging me on."

Bertha came around back of Tena and put her arms around her. "You've always been my special gift, Tena. When I was expecting you, some of the girls in the shop where I worked suggested I have an abortion. They thought I was too old."

"Oh, my God!" Tena gasped.

"Yes, terrible, but I suppose that they thought they were giving me good advice. I was over forty when I got pregnant, and Kay was nearly a grown woman. Despite me telling everyone that I was happy to be having another baby, they didn't listen. One went so far as to give me the name of a doctor who performed abortions.

"The way things went, it wasn't always easy for either of us, but I've never been sorry that God sent you along because you have brought so much joy into my life. I'm proud of you. I just don't want you to be hurt by something that you may find up there," Bertha said, sinking into the kitchen chair.

Tena caressed her mother's arm affectionately. "I know, Mom, but you don't have to worry about me."

"A mother always worries about something, and you know how I was always afraid that you would inherit your father's sickness. I want you to be happy."

"I've no interest in drinking."

"Praise God for that, at least."

"What can I say? My restless spirit is your entire fault, you know. You raised an independent daughter. Don't you remember telling me that if I were to survive in this world, I would have to toughen up? You said, 'pursue your dreams'. I don't know how tough I am, but I do know that I've inherited your resilience, Mom. I'll be okay. It's just that I get something into my head, and I have to go for it, but don't worry, I won't fall to the demon of the drink along the trail."

"I don't know what has happened with you and Ken," Bertha said softly. "You don't have to tell me unless you want to share those things."

"Thanks for understanding, Mom."

Bertha rose from the table. "I have some things that I've saved for you. I was going to give them to you a while back, but I just kept putting it off." She bent down and opened the door to the buffet cabinet. She pulled out a stack of folded linen tablecloths that hid an old brown tin box on the back of the shelf. "You know I don't believe in living in the past, but since you're so stuck on going up there to snoop around, I guess now would be a good time for me to hand these things over to you."

Tena recognized her mother's old "Budget Box".

Lifting the cover, Bertha pulled out a bulging, sealed, brown envelope. "Your father was living in a three room flat over on Clinton Avenue in Albany when he died. Kay and I went over there right after we came from the morgue the day we identified his body." She paused and stared wistfully at the package in her hand. "I found out later that he had been living in that flat since we split up, and what little furniture I found, I gave to the Salvation Army."

"I know: you told me about the furniture and that he died in jail."

"That's true. The cause of death on the death certificate is cirrhosis of the liver."

Bertha shoved the envelope into Tena's hands. "Take this before Otto comes down. He knows I was married twice before, but I told him that your father died from a heart attack. I was ashamed to tell him that Ben died in jail."

"I can understand that you would feel that way. But Otto is a kind man, and he loves you. I can't imagine that his feelings would change if he knew the truth."

Bertha narrowed her eyes as she bent to put the tin back. "Everybody doesn't have to know everything."

"Mom, my father wasn't in for murder. You don't get the electric chair for drunk driving," Tena said defensively.

"He threw his life away, and, but for the grace of God, ours might have gone with him," Bertha said sorrowfully.

"Sorry, Mom. That was a stupid comment for me to make."

"It's all right. All of it is very hard for me to think about. Inside of the envelope are your father's army discharge papers, his death certificate, our marriage license, and some old cards and photos."

Tena smoothed the envelope between her fingers. "I feel as though you have given me the key to the city."

Bertha nodded. "My giving you this envelope signifies the closing of that chapter of my life."

"Mom, thank you. Thanks also for caring enough to save it for me."

Bertha pulled a Kleenex from her apron pocket and blew her nose. After a moment of composing herself she said,

"Your father wasn't a bad man, but his sickness got out of control, and he wasted his life because of it."

Tena took a deep breath. She put her arms around her mother's shoulders and hugged her affectionately. "Have I told you how much I love your pot-roast? There's not a better Thursday night supper in all New York." She picked up her black shoulder bag from where it was draped over the corner of the chair and stuffed the envelope inside.

Bertha went into the living room and stood at the bottom of the stairs. Interjecting renewed brightness into her voice, she called up, "Hey dear, what's keeping you?"

Chapter 3

Her mouth full of toothpaste, Tena stared into her tired reflection over the bathroom sink while consoling herself that she wasn't the only woman on earth who after a failed romance handed out harmless half-truths. Masking a truth for the sake of pride is a common sin. After all, this pathway to emotional survival had long since been cleared for her by her mother who rationalized her own half-truths in such a way that they seemed harmless enough. All the same, it was becoming clear that any color lie was uncomfortable, and most especially those told to herself.

She should have told Cindy that she was devastated over Ken. Why hadn't she admitted straight out that she hadn't been merely happy with this man? Happy was far too meager a description. She relived the euphoria of his touch every night in her dreams. The whole truth was that forgetting Ken wasn't an easy order, and if she couldn't forget, how could she get on with her life? She had given up socializing after work. Somehow, what was once a stimulating, welcome breeze of catching up over a cool spritzer had lost all appeal.

Weekends she might as well be living on a deserted island. What was there to do but look forward to the solitude of her apartment, a safe place where she could be miserable without a single, chastising witness and avoid the guilt of telling half-truths. She had also begun to welcome the lonely bed that was fast becoming a private stage for past delusions. Sleep, when it finally came, sometimes provided an oasis of escape, but last night's dreaming had been very different. No island paradise last night. Oddly enough, someone else had visited, and Ken never showed. She rinsed with Listerine and shut off the bathroom light. By ten, with her mother's reluctant blessing and a few cards and photos from the past fueling her enthusiasm for this initial scouting, she was on the road driving north.

Tena held to the sincere hope that her father would have been pleased that she was anxious to become acquainted with him, even if her yearning had been seeded by the need to run away from the present. Although she could hardly remember him, she was blood of his blood, and whatever else might be wrong, she knew that this pilgrimage was right. The mysterious attraction of the modest, two hundred year old, mountain town of her ancestors was especially irresistible coming on the heels of last night's bizarre dream.

Beginning with the turn of the key in the ignition she had been replaying the previous night's odyssey, trying to make some sense out of it all, wondering how Grandma Honey had managed to usurp Ken from her secret dreamscape. She remembered that while she had talked things over with her mother, Grandma might have been mentioned, but she hadn't been thinking of her last night. Since Honey was her maternal grandmother, it struck her as odd that she would all of a sudden appear in a dream on the eve of a planned Waldron reconnection. In fact, she hadn't dreamt of her grandmother in a long time.

In the dream, Honey was once again very much alive, and the two of them were seated together on a log in the middle of a thick forest. It was a clear, bright day much like today. Tena remembered thinking that she thought that she could feel the warmth of the sun filtering down through the treetops as they laughed over something or other. While they talked, a tall man, naked except for beaver skin top hat, walked by and waved. Following behind him were six, unusually placid, gray wolves. Grandma seemed not to notice the wolves, nor did she seem the least bit put off by the stranger's nudity. She nodded and waved back, and as the man disappeared into the distant woods she began speaking about the vegetation at the bottom of their feet, pointing to thick vines that she said wound intricately around the bones of Iroquois Indian warriors. Feeling both embarrassed and fearful, Tena remembered drawing closer to her.

"Yes." Honey whispered, "This is the same trail. You must follow it."

Having made this peculiar statement, Grandma kissed her forehead, pressing a wild daisy into the palm of her hand. When she awoke Tena thought that she could smell balsam in her room. *Kay's right*, she thought. *I'm obsessed about everything.*

She glanced over at her handbag containing the newly acquired information from her mother. After she'd left her mother the previous Thursday she had raced into her apartment and opened the brown envelope. She spent half of the remainder of the evening pouring over the photos and documents her mother had given to her. One of the photos she found inside the envelope had confused her. Turning over an old black and white snapshot of three teenage boys that she guessed must have been taken sometime in the 1930's or 1940's, she had found it marked "Ben, Bob & Buck – The Waldron's Bowery – Three Hundred Acres of Heaven".

She had called her mother the next day, and when asking about these time capsules, her mom had insisted that she hadn't looked inside of the envelope for years, she didn't remember any writing on the back of the photo, and she knew nothing about any acreage either. The mention of a Bowery seemed to trigger a change in the tone of her voice, but only briefly. The conversation ended with her mother whispering into the phone, "I like my life just how it is." Tena wondered what her mother would think of Honey's visit, but on second thought, it was finally beginning to sink in that sharing last night's dream with her mother would serve no purpose. Mom cared little for living in the past.

Although she hated to admit it, her mother might have the inside track on all of this. It would be a difficult job piecing together the few paternal fragments that she brought along with her today just by walking the streets of North Creek. But, with the smallest splinter of luck, someone in North Creek might know where the New York City Bowery had an Adirondack cousin. Just where was the Waldron Bowery? The heavenly farm was the focal point of yet a much bigger mystery. She needed to know who was Ben Waldron. So many puzzles filled her mind. Who could have sent the spoon, and does it have anything at all to do with the Waldrons? After all, the inscribed *PW* could be anyone. A preconceived assumption about the why and who of the silver spoon really was foolish. She was getting a headache. *That photograph is the key; I just know it – just as I know that there is a reason for Grandma showing up in my dream last night.*

Cindy was forever talking about white light; this one, or that one's aura, and visiting angels. Tena didn't doubt for a minute that Grandma Honey was up in heaven, and still keeping a loving eye on the rest of the family as they went about the daily business of life here on earth. She wouldn't be a bit surprised if Grandma had her angel wings. She was so good to everyone, if anyone deserved to be appointed by God as an angel, it was Honey. Wouldn't it follow then that Grandma had new friends who were other angels, and that God let her borrow them once in awhile? After all, the Bible taught that angels appeared to people throughout the ages. They were messengers who helped them make decisions during difficult times.

So what would be so peculiar believing that Honey truly did indeed come to her in a vision? Hadn't she come to her that way just before she died? It was this same type of unrecognized voice that had come in the middle of the night, insisting she *go now,* a command that had whisked her back to reality and had sent her in a dazed frenzy to the hospital after Grandma had had her stroke. Without hesitating she had thrown on jeans and a sweater and driven the nearly thirty miles in a snowstorm to be at her grandmother's bedside. When she arrived she had been shocked to find her unconscious. She had never told anyone, but in the still of that hospital room, just before dawn, she had been convinced that her grandmother had said, "Goodbye, beauty girl." Her lips never moved, but Tena was sure she had heard her. Now, what else could she think except that Honey had truly touched her once again? It had to be that Honey wanted her to know she was doing the right thing today. She found herself recalling something else Grandma once told her. "I like thinking that the Lord is holding my hand," Honey had said one evening while they sat together rocking on the front porch swing. Sometimes I think I can hear Him as clear as the buzzer on the oven." Tena smiled thinking of her grandmother's infectious laugh. "Don't be afraid to listen to your heart, dear, Grandma urged. "Being able to hear, truly hear, is a wonderful gift from God."

Tena wondered if her father had lived would they have bonded the way she had done with Grandma Honey, or Kay had with her own dad. Her sister was the fortunate one to have known her father's love. They had thirteen years together before her father was killed in the accident at the mill. She thought it very special when Kay would say that she still sometimes imagined that she could smell the aroma of his pipe tobacco, or that she couldn't watch a football game on television with Jake without thinking of her dad. Always there was a jar of rock candy, Kay's father's favorite, in their cupboard. Kay and Jen loved it.

Tena thought about the DNA article she had read recently, and the fascinating theory that people inherit DNA from ancestors who had lived thousands of years before; she need not confirm a thousand years ago, just one generation back would do.

What am I supposed to hear now?

Her thoughts turned toward happier childhood times of pretending she could fly like Peter Pan and trapping bear like Davy Crockett. She smiled to herself, thinking of her furry raccoon hat and the wild frontier make-believe world that she had built in the long front hallway of their old house where her mother had rented the downstairs flat, remembering too the invisible bear that had became a best friend after she had 'caught' him in an old shoebox. Kay would be quick enough to tease her about her make-believe worlds, but her mother would laugh and wave Kay aside, insisting a child's imagination was a blessing that faded all too soon. How true, Tena thought.

During the week she had gone to the local library, pulling several books from the New York State history section. In the reference section she looked up the definition of the word, "bowery". She had discovered that the Dutch colonists called their big northern farms *boweries.*

Thinking about the photograph, Tena wished it were a better one since she and her mother believed that one of the boys was her father, but the shot had been taken from a distance, and the boy's faces were shadowed. *Who were these three friends, and where was this place they loved so much that they described it as "heaven"?*

As she drove along she made a mental inventory of the items of antiquity in her mother's house. Her mother wasn't kidding when she said that she didn't believe in living in the past; there were few antiques housed over on Grand Avenue. Great-Grandfather Clem LaCross' beaver-skinned top hat, said to have been passed down from the grandson of a French fur trader by the name of LaCroix, was displayed at the bottom of the curio cabinet, and Grandma Honey's pair of gorgeous, lace-overlay vases were on the top shelf, but that was it. Of course, there were her old, two-blade ice skates that hung in the mudroom, bringing back memories not only of skating at the flooded Lincoln Park ball park but also of the overcrowded public swimming pool. One thing she could hear for sure was the scream of the lifeguard's whistle piercing her eardrums every five minutes.

Her mother talked about his alcoholism, expressed regret for not being able to help him, and at such times Tena could see the sorrow that crept into her mom's eyes. Even though her mother didn't stay with her father, it was clear that something about him had captured her heart. *My parents were opposites right from the start. What is this man-woman thing supposed to be? I didn't make Ken happy. Mom couldn't help my father, and so far I can't find a guy that's right for me. Maybe there isn't one. No, I just have to be patient. And besides, I have places to go and things to do.*

Today, though the air was muggy, her leather seat seemed less sticky, recalling night ice skating on the park's flooded, frozen ball field, the wintry ice reflecting the illumination of the streetlights that came on near five in the evening. How often had she been scolded for lingering at the park when supper grew cold? She visualized her block—Suzie Robert's three-story brownstone house, Pat's Corner Store where Grandma Honey selected dill pickles for purchase straight from the big wooden barrel, the firehouse with the firemen sitting around outside, and DeMarco's front stoop where Jim DeMarco sat telling Italian jokes which made his wife furious. Tena could still hear the whooping firehouse alarm and the thunder of the engines taking off within a breath of the doors going up

Pickles, Tena thought. *You just can't find pickles like those anymore.* What was it that Grandma Honey used to say, oh yes: *Pickles are like friends, some real sweet, and some real bitter. Careful how you pick 'em.*

The clock in the town hall's tower chimed noon as Tena entered North Creek. She proceeded slowly along the street where nearly twenty years before she had attended her father's funeral while holding her mother's hand. Vaguely her memory conjured up the big white hotel that she believed would be at the end of the town, as well as the funeral parlor that was mounted on the top of the steep hill in front of her. A chill ran down her back as she pictured an American flag being folded neatly into a triangle. She recalled the sound of taps, and a uniformed man who placed that flag solemnly into her mother's arms. She remembered her mother's tears.

The business section for this centuries-old Adirondack settlement was comprised of four or five city blocks – no McDonalds, no Pizza Hut, no parking lots, just single rows of three-story, wood fronted buildings stuck endlessly together on each side of the main street. She passed a few bars, but it looked as if the place called "Rogers Restaurant and Tavern" would be the only option for lunch. She didn't mind that her father came from small town America and not a big metropolitan area, or even a small city. This was an advantage for her investigation. Maybe someone would remember the Waldron family, though she acknowledged that it had been thirty years or more since Ben Waldron had lived in this area.

Tena parked a block away from Rogers, put two nickels into the meter, and walked up Broad Street's steep hill passing Kelly's Funeral Home and J&B Hardware. She paused under the shade of Rees Dress Shop's bright yellow, canvass awning to peek through the glass storefront window at the sportily dressed mannequins. It seemed as if it wasn't any cooler up north amid the great pines than it was sitting in her cramped office at the <u>Record</u>. By the time she reached Rogers Restaurant she was perspiring so much that her blouse was stuck to her back.

There were two entrances into the Rogers establishment – one had a hand painted sign marked "Bar" over the doorway. The other sign over the adjacent entrance read "Restaurant". Tena pulled open the latter door and found herself in a large room scattered with small tables covered with red-checked cloths. But, the funny thing was that both doors actually led into the same room. A tall, balding man in his forties was behind the curved mahogany bar drying glasses. He was engaged in conversation with two older men in overalls. The three stopped talking and nodded a greeting in her direction as she found a table.

"Pretty hot day out there," the bartender called over. "Can I get you something young lady?"

"Just a soda." She felt uncomfortable.

The reply was upbeat and friendly. "I'm alone today. My girl called in sick, so I'm it. Can I interest you in an ice cold coke in one of our frosted mugs?"

"Thank you, that sounds great. I'm sorry about your waitress."

The two other patrons chuckled. "You got that right girly," the one with the beard said.

Squirming in her seat, she tried to figure out what he meant.

The bartender walked toward her table. "Don't pay any attention to those two old birds," he said placing her soft drink in front of her. "They love to dish it out. That's what happens when you're retired, and don't have anything better to do than to bother nice young ladies." He glanced up toward the bar adding, "The heat must be getting to them."

"Old Birds are we now. Hey, Larry, you're not so young yourself anymore."

"Touchy aren't we today," Larry retaliated good-naturedly, returning to the bar.

"Another few years you'll be sittin' on this side of the bar with us."

"Sure, Sure."

"Maybe we should go someplace else where our company is more appreciated."

Larry ignored them. "Is your coke ok, Miss?"

Tena smiled. "Yes, nice and cold."

"I've got some good boiled ham. I could make you a ham and cheese on rye bread."

"Yes, please. That sounds great."

The bearded man swung around on his stool to face Tena. "Are ya just up for a visit?"

Tena hesitated. "Sort of."

The old man nodded. "Pretty soon we'll have all kinds of folks wandering all over the place around here. It's quiet today, but all heck is gonna break loose before ya know it. Folks that own camps will be opening them up all around the lake soon. The motels fill up. If Pat Landry over at our Chamber of Commerce office has his way this year we'll have more tourists than black flies. I blame it on all that damn advertising he does in those New York City papers."

His companion added, "The dang black flies are worse this June than I ever saw 'em. He called over his shoulder in Tena's direction, "Best you stay where it's screened in or go down and buy some of that bug repellent at the drug store."

Larry agreed. "He's right. The pests started extra early this year. My wife complains that it makes no sense to plant anything since she can't enjoy her garden. All things considered, I think North Creek is a better winter resort than a summer place, these last few years especially, ever since they opened the ski lodge and they put musical entertainment on the trains. Out of town folks really like the sing-a-longs. Of course, my wife doesn't like to hear me say so."

The bearded man said, "We 'Old Birds' fly south with our wives under our wings the first sign of snow, and our women are happy to get out of here because, when that bunch comes in, they're too much to live by."

Tena detected more than a tinge of bitterness in his voice. "I don't ski much," she said, "and I'm really not a total tourist. I'm here to look up my dad's family."

The two elderly men shook their heads and murmured. "Looks like we have another seeker."

"What's your dad's name?" the bartender asked as he brought over her sandwich.

"His name was Ben Waldron. He passed away a long time ago, but he was born in this town, and he lived here till he went into the army during World War Two."

"Either of you guys ever heard of him?" Larry asked, placing the sandwich on the table in front of Tena. "You both have been around since Noah's flood."

"No, I never heard of a Ben Waldron, but there's that lady up there in the nursing home with my Emma's mother. Her last name is Waldron. Don't you remember Larry? They had her picture in the paper a couple of Sundays ago when she turned ninety-six. She's in good shape for an old gal, and she had quite a life according to the newspaper article. She taught school in Albany early on and then taught in this area. She was even in China years ago and wrote a couple of books. Her name is Tess Waldron."

Tena could feel her knees shaking. "I wonder if that could be the aunt that my mother talked about."

"You think so?" the bartender mused.

A flutter of excitement ran through her. *Could she possibly have driven into town and within an hour found a blood relative?*

Digging into her handbag she said, "I have a photograph. Maybe one of you would recognize the boys in the picture?"

She walked over and placed the snapshot on the bar. All three heads came together as they studied the faces of the friends from the past.

"I'll be danged, that one young fellow looks like Buck, doesn't he Earl?"

Earl put on his glasses. "He sure does, but it's hard telling since I didn't know Buck back then."

"Buck who?" Tena asked

"Buck Van Ness," Earl replied.

"Oh, gosh, I wish I could talk with him. Where does Mr. Van Ness live?"

"Died last fall," the bartender stated flatly.

"Yeah, too bad about Buck," Earl interjected. "He was a good bowler, threw a heck of a ball."

Earl picked up the picture to look it over more carefully. "I wouldn't know those other two boys, but my wife, Emma, might. She grew up in this town; me and my friend here come from Weavertown."

Tena was about to ask about Emma when Earl suggested, "You should go up to Garnet Manor House and see that Tess Waldron."

Tena smiled "Guess my next stop has to be Garnet Manor House. Where is it?"

Earl walked over to the window. "If you go up this street one block and turn right and then keep on going up the hill on Normal Street, another four blocks and you'll be there. You can't miss the place."

"Thanks gentlemen. You've been a big help to me." Tena returned to her seat, finished her sandwich, and drained the last bit of her Coke.

"Glad I could help you out. Good luck to you, Miss."

Tena paid her check and gathered up her things.

"Be sure to come back and let us know how you did," Larry said.

"I will."

Chapter 4

Garnet Manor House for the Aged sat grandly on the summit of Rock Hill overlooking the old Adirondack logging and mining town. During the latter part of the nineteenth century, deep pits dug tenaciously into the earth yielded garnet gemstones from crystalline used primarily for the sand paper industry. Now, like the glittering tiara of a surviving nineteenth century queen, the freshly painted yellow gables of the home sparkled down upon North Creek's clean storefronts where clever little signs over sweetheart arbors beckoned tourists.

Although the Barton Mines continued, the function of the big white house that once resounded with the brash male voices of boarders had changed. Gone are the Irish miners, and no longer does cook Bridgett Mahoney await the shrill six o'clock whistle to set down plates. Gone too is the rattle of the miners' empty, tin lunch boxes as the workers plodded wearily up the path toward the bucket of water and bar of lye soap that waited by the back door.

But, the graceful Victorian structure that the mine workers called home has not lost a bit of its charm or usefulness. The building still displays an opulent second level veranda that is swung all around the front. The high porch continues to be a safe platform for viewing life on the grassy lawns below.

Recalling old stories of how Bridgett used to tie a fly swatter to her rather round waist, today the old men chuckle while rocking in the wicker chairs. The resident ladies good-naturedly tell them to *go on with themselves* while praising the Lord for the comfort of the double-seated, well-cushioned, wooden swings. Someone suggests that Bridgette wasn't the cook's name at all, going on to say that all Irish women who cooked for a living were often called Bridgette. One, small, poetic voice in the group muses that the bright furniture amid the wicker on this massive, gray painted porch gives an appearance of overgrown poppies blooming out of a foggy bed. The old men laugh all the harder.

Full of anticipation, Tena was soon in the midst of this hodgepodge of well-ripened commentators. Introducing herself at the front door to a petite, middle-aged woman who was neatly dressed in a light orchid colored suit, immediately she was invited in and asked to take a seat in the parlor, where she quickly found a comfortable, red velvet, winged-back chair. After a few moments of pleasantries, an attendant was dispatched to see if Tess Waldron was feeling up to visitors.

Soaking in further details of the room, Tena noticed, scattered about the parlor, several women residents who were seemingly swallowed up within the plush cushions of the tapestry sofas. The women were engrossed in a television game show, arguing over possible correct answers to the questions presented to contestants. A few feet away, two men played chess, indifferent to the squabbling of their feminine companions. An ornate, round, mahogany table that shone like a gemstone held one of the largest floral arrangements that Tena had ever seen: a large earthenware vase filled with wild Adirondack ferns interwoven with yellow and white longstem roses.

It wasn't long before a frail, white-haired woman in a rose colored dress was wheeled toward her. The fine line of her demure smile was softly enhanced by a light pink lipstick.

Turning toward Tena, the attendant whispered, "She's having a good day today, so I'm sure you'll both have a very nice visit."

The caretaker bent to speak into Tess Waldron's ear. "Now, if it's all right I'm going to leave the two of you nice people together, but if you need anything, just let Kelly know."

Squinting blue eyes appraised Tena carefully. "You must be Chub's girl," cheerful lips whispered triumphantly after only a brief examination.

Startled, Tena replied, "I beg your pardon?"

The woman leaned forward in her wheelchair. "Well, I declare that you look just like Benny. What I mean to say is that you look just like Ben Waldron, though I imagine you were thinking that I was implying that you're fat. Benny wasn't fat either when he grew up, but he was a butterball when he was a little fellow. Chubs was what we all called Benny as a boy. I called him that when he was a grown man. He would get so embarrassed."

She wheeled herself closer. "I suppose that you know that I'm Tess Waldron and I'm ninety-six years young."

Tena felt like a soaring kite. "I'm so pleased to meet you. I think we may be related. I'm Tena Waldron. My father was Ben Waldron."

"I'm a little hard of hearing. You said you're Tena Waldron?"

"Yes, I'm Tena with the letter e, as opposed to the spelling of the name the other way, T-I-N-A. My mother said that my father named me," Tena stammered uncomfortably.

Tess confidently nodded affirmation. "I am very pleased to make your acquaintance. And, please honey, sit back down. You know, I'm always so happy to have family come visit me. There's not so many of us left anymore."

"Family?" Tena reached out numbly toward the woman who was indeed her great-aunt. Their fingers touched and she thought for a moment that she would foolishly burst into tears. She took a deep breath. She didn't want to look stupid or act sappy. "I'm so happy to meet you. Should I call you Aunt?"

"I would be delighted if you would do so. If your father was Ben Waldron, then I'm your Aunt, and deary, I do not doubt for one minute that Benny was your father. I don't hear a thimble's worth without my hearing aid, but my sight is still excellent. Goodness, it looks to me like he spit you right out. I can tell you something else," Tess paused for a moment, clearing her throat, "I know all about how you must have gotten your name. Your daddy must have found that name written in the family Bible."

"Really," Tena said, bursting with curiosity.

"I would think so. Your Grandpa and Grandma loved the Lord and kept to the Word. But I remember their bible very well because of all that was written in was so interesting. It had to be nearly two hundred years old."

"You know my mother did say that my father named me for someone in the Waldron family."

"Yes, dear, and yours is a very old name. One of the first Waldron settlers to sail from Holland and put down roots in this country with her husband and children in the New York

Colonies was a woman by the name of Tennake. They lived in New York City, which back then was called New Amsterdam. As a matter of fact, I think that way back one of your great-great-grandmothers was called Tena. Benny must have had all of that in mind when he named you."

Sinking into the wingchair, Tena was almost afraid to believe her ears.

Tess continued. "When I was young the families used to amuse each other with the Old Dutch tales around here. Everyone enjoyed those old time fairy tales as much as the true historical sagas. Delightful, mischievous, Dutch characters like silly Rip Van Winkle, who fell asleep under the bridge for twenty years, completely enchanted us."

As Tena sat listening she thought that she must be moving around in one of her dreams. "I can't believe I've found you," she said.

"Well, I've been here a long time, and I'm kind of surprised it took you so long to find me, but the Good Lord has everything come along in His perfect timing. He always finds a way to help us out with whatever it is that we are trying to accomplish. So tell me, did you come on account of the newspaper story that was done about me?" Tess asked proudly.

After a moment Tena remembered what she had heard earlier. "No, I really didn't. What happened was that I was at the restaurant in town, and a man there told me about you having your picture in the paper a few weeks ago, but I really came up to North Creek on my own. I was curious about my father's hometown. I didn't know anything about your picture before I had lunch. I hope you will forgive me for just barging in like this, but I was so anxious to see if you really were my father's aunt. You see, I never really knew my dad because he and my mother were separated when I was a young child."

"That must have been hard on you. It doesn't surprise me that much though that he'd have difficulty getting along with a wife because from early on Benny was a fellow that the devil would like to pester. He carried a heavy cross, and I think the War, and all he went through over there, was all too much on him. Those poor boys that went over there had an awful ordeal to endure. God bless them."

Pausing again to clear her throat, the older woman reflected, "They all had to be so far from home and see all those terrible things. It must have been horrible. But then again, Benny was a strange little boy. Still, even though he was a peculiar little duck, I was always fond of him," she sighed.

Tena clasped moist hands together in her lap.

"Do you remember your father at all?" Tess asked gently.

"I remember coming up here for his funeral with my mother, but not much more. Were you at his funeral, Aunt Tess?"

Twisting her ring around for a moment before she replied, Tess responded. "No, I wasn't here, unfortunately. I was in England for a few years back in the fifties. I did some missionary work after the war, and taught over there. My brother, Herb, wrote to me that Benny had passed away, and I would have written to your mother when I came back to the States, but none of us had her address. I think though that Betty – that would be Herb's first wife – had a letter from your mother."

"We must have moved by then."

"Yes, I imagine. I met your mother once or twice before I left for England. I think we met at Esther Hughes's wedding. Is your mother still alive, I hope?"

"Yes, she is. Mom is remarried for many years now. My stepfather's name is Otto Pollack. He's a good man. She's very happy."

"Oh, I'm glad for her," Tess said gently. "Give her my regards when you see her, will you? And you must encourage her to come along and visit me soon."

"I will do that."

Tess observed the women who were quieter now that their television program had gone off. She tried to reposition herself in the wheelchair with her back to them. Drifting back into conversation, Tess said, "before my hair went all white, I used to have red hair, just the color of yours. I took a lot of teasing when I was a girl over my red hair and freckles. Do you get teased?"

"Not anymore, but I gave Mike Poma a black eye about it when I was in the fifth grade," Tena giggled.

Tess laughed. "Well, I wanted to give out a few black eyes in my time, too."

Tena liked her newly found relative. She drew herself up and sat on the edge of her chair. "I have a thousand questions, but right now I want to ask just one."

"Ask whatever you wish."

Tena pulled out the creased black and white snapshot. "I have a picture I'd like you to look at because I really don't know for sure who the boys in it might be. I think that one of the boys is my father, and the other is possibly my uncle."

"Hold it up close to me, will you?"

Tena did so.

"Oh, sure, I know who they all are. That's your father, his big brother, Bob, and the Van Ness boy, the one they called Buckie," she said while pointing to each. "Bob and that Van Ness boy used to drag your father all over with them. I remember that well enough. Hank, that was your grandfather, was always at Bob to take Chubs along. Bob would get mad and make a face, but off they would all go."

Tena flipped over the photo. "There is something written on the back. It says 'Waldron's Bowery'."

"Probably was taken by Hank at the Bowery."

Tena said, "Where was that? They must have liked it. See, they say its heaven."

"That was your grandfather's farm, and back then the old place was as what we all imagined Heaven must be like," Tess answered squarely. "It was a big farm, well over three-hundred acres. Ivan, Hanks father, being the eldest son, inherited it from his people. The farm was passed down through the generations starting from the Hollander settlers who came up to Elm Hill from the southern part of New York to the Adirondacks. Way back, North Creek was nothing but trees and Indians. The first Waldron in the area was William Waldron who was married to a Norwegian girl, Judah Bradt. That Tennake I just told you about, though, married into the Waldrons long before Judah, and she was the ancestral grandmother to everyone."

Obviously tired, Tess paused. Tena asked, "Can't I get you a glass or water or something, or would you like me to call the attendant?"

"No dear, I'm all right. It's good to have someone to talk with about old times. As I said, we all loved to tell stories, and Ivan's favorite was about his ancestors. It was Ivan, a great one for history, who told us that those North Creek Waldrons descended from the people who came over on the ships in the mid-sixteen hundreds. He called them the original American pioneers!"

"American pioneers?" Tena was fascinated.

"As I recall, Will Waldron, an early settler, built a one room log cabin on the same spot as a century later they built the farm. Later, the family sold that farm and there was another that Ivan called his "Heavenly Bowery." He had a sign painted and hung it on the front fence. Oh, goodness, I went to some hum-ding picnics there. He raised mostly milk cows, had a marvelous team of six mules, as I recall, and a goose that acted more like a watchdog. That goose was terrible. He used to have to put it in the barn when anyone came to visit."

Tena laughed. "Sounds like he loved the farm."

"That he did. And, those farm products back then were the real McCoy. In those days you drank what the cow gave you: real milk, none of this diluted watery stuff they sell in the markets nowadays."

Tena, said, "My mother's uncle had a farm, and she and her brothers and sisters used to spend two weeks there in the summer. Mom loved it. She's told me that she used to come back home six pounds fatter."

"Yes, that homemade ice cream would do the trick," Tess agreed.

"Sounds to me like my great-grandfather wanted the world to know how much he loved his home."

Tess's lips curled into a smile. "Yes, Ivan had a flare for showmanship to be sure. He was a grand gentleman, a bit of a romantic. An odd combination, wouldn't you say…a farmer who is a romantic?"

"I don't know," Tena mused. "I've always thought that there is something romantic about the landscape of the countryside."

Tess said, "I'll tell you something that most folks don't know about me, I was born a Murphy. I married Ivan's younger brother, Pete, but after only a few years of wedded bliss, my husband died from leukemia. He was only twenty-eight."

Tena's face registered sadness. "I'm sorry."

Tess shrugged her shoulders. "Don't be sorry. It all happened a long time ago. Anyway, I was telling you about your father."

"My mother didn't know anything about a farm up here. She told me that my father worked for the railroad."

"I suppose things go the way the Lord wants them to go," Tess said, staring down at her pink lacquered fingernails.

"That's my mother's philosophy."

Tess nodded her agreement. "The War changed many lives. When the fighting ended the young men went into the cities to find jobs. It might have been that the pay was better than working in the mines or struggling with the difficult North Country land."

Tena recalled how her mother complained that the War was responsible for her father's drinking.

"I guess I should be happy that he left North Creek," Tena said. "If he hadn't, he and my mother would never have met."

Tess smiled. "Did you know that you had a grandmother who could trace her lineage to the Indians? Your father took much teasing over that grandmother story."

"Do you think that's why he was so secretive about his family with my mother?"

"Do you mean something he wanted to hide?"

"Possibly."

"No, dear, I think he just saw opportunity elsewhere. He wanted to start fresh. The War was over, the folks gone, and soon the land was gone too. That was all."

"Mom never believed him about being part Indian."

Tess chuckled. "Everybody who has roots up in this part of the world has a good chance of being related to the Old Dutch, the Old New Englanders, or the Old Indians."

A blonde woman attendant came by to ask if Tess wanted her tea along with a few cookies. She politely asked Tena if she would also like some. "Yes, that would be wonderful," Tena quickly answered.

"Tea for two coming right up."

Tena turned to her aunt. "Aunt Tess, whatever happened to Ivan's farm?"

Tess sighed, "Ivan went to his reward some years ago and left everything to his son, Henry. Your father and his brother, Bob, inherited the place when your grandfather, Hank, passed on." She paused reflectively, and for a second, Tena thought that was going to be the extent of the information offered.

However, Tess continued, "Your father resembled his father a great deal. He was very tall as was Hank."

Tena smiled.

"Hank was a carpenter when not working the farm; he built many of the homes up about these parts. In answer to your question, my brother told me that your father and Bob, who would be your uncle, sold the land right after the War to the company that built that big skiing lodge. Not that folks didn't come to snow ski way back before the War; you know the tourists have been coming up here for years on the train from New York City. Those city folk like to think that they're in the wilderness when they come up. They pay an awful lot of money, in my opinion, just to slide down the side of the mountain in the snow and have a bed to rest their bones in afterwards. But, as I was saying, the new lodge was a different kind of resort from anything that had been here before. Of course, the worst tragedy of all was that the old farmhouse that belonged to the Waldrons for all those years got torn down. It was a pity. Nowadays, folks play golf where we held our family picnics."

Tess paused as a male attendant with shoulder length brown hair appeared carrying two cups of tea, sugar packets, a small pitcher of cream, and a plate of cookies on a small tray covered with paper doilies. "I'll set this down right here on the coffee table for you ladies. Watch, it might be hot though," he cautioned.

"Thank you, Tommy," Tess called after him.

"You enjoy it now," Tommy called over his shoulder.

"He's such a nice lad, but his father should insist he get a haircut."

"Can I fix your tea for you," Tena asked.

"Just a little cream, if you don't mind. Thank you."

"He does seem pleasant," Tena said.

"Yes, he is, and all in all, it's really not so bad living here. It was hard in the beginning not having my privacy all the time, but generally I'm used to it now."

"That's good."

"You know, Tena, Tess added sheepishly, it's queer that you've come to visit me out of the blue, right after your brother, Johnny, has come."

Tena bolted upright, nearly spilling the hot tea in her lap. The teacup rattled in her hands. "Aunt Tess, I don't have a brother." She could barely hear herself talk for the roar of confusion in her head.

Tess sipped her tea cautiously, her face wrinkled up in thought. Finally she replaced the cup into the saucer and placed it on the end table. She looked at the young woman in front of her inquisitively. "You don't know anything about John?

"No, nothing," Tena answered bewildered.

"Oh my word, I suppose that he would be a half-brother to you, seeing how he's Ava's boy. Ava was your father's first wife."

Tena's eyes widened, she could barely register what she was hearing. "First wife?"

"Oh, goodness, I can see that I've let a cat out of the bag. I shouldn't have said anything. I can see that from the look on your face. How foolish of me. If you don't know anything about Johnny, I guess you wouldn't know about Ava either, would you?" Tess's drooping, milk-white cheeks suddenly produced a hue of color.

Tena put her cup down. She had lost all desire for her tea. "Don't be sorry, really; no harm is done. It's only that I'm surprised because I don't think my mother knew of his first marriage either. I'm sure if she knew, she would have told me," she said soothingly while thinking, *this must be my week for bombs.*

Tess leaned over and patted her hand. "Well, I'll tell you what happened as far as I know it to be. After the war, your father came home to North Creek and to Ava, who was his wife then, but she had gotten tired of waiting for him. From what I heard, he opened the front door to their flat and the closet was filled with another man's clothes. Needless to say, your poor father was brokenhearted and, of course, he got very mad."

"There can't be anything worse than that kind of deceit," Tena mumbled sourly.

"I imagine not," Tess replied. "Still, it's not right to judge another. I always imagined that Ava didn't have the heart to send him a Dear John letter while he was overseas, so he had no idea that everything had changed while he was gone. He had thought that he'd surprise her, but it was he who got the big surprise."

Tena felt sick. "How painful that must have been for him."

"Yes, I'm sure that it was, but I hear tell that he wasn't alone because that sort of thing happened to many lads back then. Sometimes wives didn't know if their husbands were dead or alive. When the boys were at the front, a soldier's family back home wouldn't hear from them for months on end, and, of course, the men were usually gone for years. Loneliness, I'm sure, weakened many good people."

The blonde woman stopped in front of them. "Are you getting tired, Tess?"

"No, I'm just fine"

The woman stood over her for a minute, observing her dubiously. "You'll let me know, Ok?"

"I will let you know."

The attendant retreated. "They mean well, but sometimes they are all a big pain."

Tena hardly heard the complaint. She was wilted. "I can't believe all of this," she whispered.

"Oh, it's all true," Tess said with renewed spryness. "It is apparent that he loved Ava in those days because, you know, he forgave her and they got back together, but my understanding was that their reunion was short lived. I heard that after a month or two they separated. She must have been expecting at the time."

Tena studied Tess, wondering how much of this was fact, and how much was fiction. She was an elderly woman. She might be confused. Still, she needed to hear the ending so that she could try to piece things together. "What happened then to Ava?"

"Oh, well, let's see," Tess said. "She took off and nobody saw her for a number of years. I think by then your father and Ava were divorced."

"Thank God for that much," Tena mused nervously.

Tess didn't seem to hear, and Tena could tell she was growing tired. "We didn't see much of your father either, come to think of it, although he did bring your mother to the wedding, where as I said before, I met her. I do remember that quite well."

"So...you never saw Ava again?"

Tess appeared pensive, "She showed up one other time in the early sixties as I recall. She was living with her little Johnny over in Johnsonville. Some years after Benjamin died she brought him to my brother Herbert's house where I was staying for awhile, so we all had the opportunity of meeting Ben's boy. Johnny was still young, and I remember him as being a well-mannered child," Tess paused. "My brother and I lived together for a number of years on and off. After Herb passed, I came to Garnet Manor."

"Was Ava still with the man?"

"Well, I know she remarried, but I don't think he was the man she was involved with when your father came back. I don't know much about anything that happened around here during those early years after the war because I wasn't in the States much in those days.

As I recall, Ava and her husband were killed in a car crash some time ago. His stepfather adopted Johnny and he goes by his last name, which is Van Ness. He told me that his mother's sister raised him after the accident."

"How terrible," Tena said.

"And Johnny has visited you recently?"

Tess nodded. "Yes, I had not seen him since that one time so many years before, and I didn't have any idea who he was when he came by. He's quite good-looking, but not tall like Ben. He has more his mother's coloring with her wavy hair and those unique violet-blue eyes. He told me that he lives down near Kingston."

Tena sighed. *She had told her mother not to worry, that she was a big girl prepared for anything, but this whole saga had knocked her for a loop. She wasn't prepared for this...not at all.*

"I don't know what to say Aunt Tess. All of this is such a surprise. Why did he come to see you after all of this time?"

"Probably like you he got a notion it was time to see what there was about his other half – the Waldron relatives, and I'm about all that's left up here. Who knows why we walk this way or that way, but it is good to know that the Almighty has us all in the palm of his hand."

"Yes of course, but it sure is odd that we both started walking the same path at the same time."

"I suppose."

Tena took hold of Tess's frail hands, which were cool to the touch, but the elder woman's eyes were full of warmth. "I should be leaving, but I can't tell you how much this visit and all that you have told me means."

"Tena, I'm so happy that you came, and I hope you will come again."

"I will," Tena promised. "I've planned a vacation up here soon."

"Good!" Tess responded enthusiastically.

The blonde sentinel had returned. "I saw you yawn, Tess. I think it would be best if you took a little rest now." Her tone was kind, but firm.

Tena stood, "I was just leaving," she said standing. "I'll phone ahead the next time, and I'll try to come again in a few weeks, but in-between you take care of yourself."

Tess smiled. "I will do that, and you do the same. I'll be waiting for your call."

Chapter 5

The sky was black as Tena drove away from the nursing home parking lot; the heavens opening up full throttle by the time she had reached home. Dashing for her building she barely remembered the long drive back. Her mind was still in an absolute whirl.

Inside, she immediately noticed the shutdown sign that Jimmy, their building super, had placed in the hallway in front of the elevator. There must have been another outage, she thought while heading for the stairwell that was lit by emergency lighting. Once in front of her apartment door, she struggled to get her key into the lock, all the while hearing the telephone ringing. Finally in, breathless and annoyed that the faulty lockset hadn't been changed as Jimmy had promised, she grabbed the receiver. "Hello"

"Tena? Where on earth have you been roaming? Ma's half crazy over there. She has been calling you all afternoon. She's frantic that her baby girl was caught in this wild downpour and ran the car off the road, or something worse," Kay said, her voice oscillating between hysteria and condemnation.

"What? Mom knew that I was going out of town today. She must have forgotten that North Creek isn't just around the corner. I just got in this second. You won't believe what I have to tell you."

"Okay, slow down. What about North Creek? You didn't tell me anything about going up there when I called you on your birthday – did you? Anyway, I'm glad you're back safe and sound, and I suggest that you call Ma right away, Teeny. She's so worried."

"For Pete's sake, Kay, Mom drives me nuts sometimes."

"She loves you, and we all drive each other nuts sometimes," Kay responded dryly. "But, call her anyway."

Tena kicked off her penny loafers. "For that matter, yes, I'm sure that I told you I was going up there. You should have reminded Mom of how far north I was going and set her mind to rest, but then again, sometimes it seems that neither of you listen to a word I have to say."

Obviously annoyed, Kay snapped back. "What's the matter with you? I always listen to you. Don't be so dramatic. With all that's going on with Florida, and the drive down and back, I'm happy to remember my name. So I forgot, that's all, and okay, I'm sorry, but you need to call Ma."

"I'll call. I don't want her upset either, but she does worry needlessly."

Kay's voice calmed. "Well, she doesn't see it that way, so you had better give her a buzz, or she'll have the State Police combing the highways for you."

"I promise, the minute I hang up I will. You know, I'm surprised to hear your voice. You're back sooner than I thought."

"We got in around two," Kay said. "Rest assured, I'll never go down in June again. The heat in Tampa was steamy. Jake can go if he wants. Your brother-in-law loves the sun, but not me. I find..."

Tena couldn't keep still another minute. "Kay, did you know that my father was married before he married, Mom?"

"What are you talking about?"

"You couldn't imagine what kind of a day I had today. As I said, I went to North Creek, and to make a long story short, I met this woman who is my Great Aunt."

"On Ben's side, I'm assuming?"

"Yes, of course, on my father's side." Tena heard Kay sigh.

Tena continued, "Let me back up a little. Last Thursday, when I went over to Mom's for dinner, she gave me this big manila envelope that I'd never seen before. It's full of things that had belonged to my father."

"So?" Kay interjected impatiently.

"So...that's why I couldn't put off going up there anymore."

"Teeny, how could this woman be related? Any aunt of Ben's would be a hundred years old."

"Well, she claims to be ninety-six, but maybe she exaggerates because I'll tell you, she seems as sharp as a tack."

Tena held the receiver under her chin as she pulled a package of bologna and another of American cheese from the refrigerator. She slapped the sliced cold cuts between two slices of rye. "Get this, she told me that I have a brother!"

"What!"

"I swear to you. I'm telling you exactly as she told me. His name is Johnny Van Ness."

Kay said, "Let me get this straight. You went off on one of your mysterious jaunts, met someone who is practically a centenarian who claims to be your aunt, and now you have a brother. Teeny, be realistic: this is the real world I'm talking about now. Don't you think that if you had a brother, I would know about him? You don't have a brother, honey, and you're stuck with me as your only sister."

"So you don't know anything? You're telling me the truth about this?"

"I swear that I don't remember anything about what Ben did before he married Ma. I don't want to hurt you, Teeny, but I think your father was a man with a plate full of secrets. Still and all, I think a brother is kind of hard to hide from everyone; wouldn't you say?"

"You don't think Mom has secrets that she'll take to the grave?"

"Well, maybe that's where whatever it is should be—buried. She would have told me," Kay persisted.

Tena found her euphoric high drop. "Why would Tess Waldron make up such a story if it weren't true?"

Kay cleared her throat. "Elderly people are often lonely, and when people are lonely they crave attention. On the other hand, I think I am remembering now that it is true that Ben had an Aunt Tessie, so I suppose there is a possibility that this woman is who she claims, but the rest is nonsense."

Tena sighed out her frustration. "I'm going to ask Mom. I'll call her now to let her know that I'm all right, but I won't mention anything about this on the phone. I want to tell her this story face to face."

"Good."

"I am confronting her, but I'll sleep on all of this first."

"Seriously, be gentle. Remember, you really don't know what's what, so don't make her any more nervous than she is already with Jake and me talking about the Florida property. How did you come to talk with this woman to begin with?"

"That's another odd thing: did you ever feel that something was supposed to happen, and then it did?"

"Oh, God, here we go."

"No, really. Cindy said something like that to me last week while we were at lunch. Well, never mind about that. Actually, some men at a bar where I stopped for lunch directed me to the nursing home where Tess lives."

"Oh, Glory! This gets better all the time."

"It's not how it sounds," Tena said defensively.

"Does all this somehow have something to do with Ken? Ma thinks you broke up with him. Did you?"

Tena let out another sigh. "I broke it off. We're done."

"For good?"

"I told him I don't want to see him. I'm trying to stick to my guns, and I will, but it hurts. Ken's another reason why I thought it would be helpful for me to take a ride out of here for a day."

"That was probably best."

"That's what I'm trying to do...just whatever is best to get over him. I don't know, maybe I'll never meet the right guy."

"I'm sorry you're hurting, but you're wrong. You will meet someone someday who will be perfect for you, and when you do, you're going to wonder why you ever gave Ken the time of day."

"Sure hope so."

"I know so. Trouble with you is that you never wanted to look at anyone else for the past three years. I tried to fix you up a couple of times when you broke it off with Ken before. Remember, Rachael's brother?"

"Kay, I've told you, Sam is very nice, but he isn't my type."

"How would you know? You hardly spoke to him that evening."

"We spoke."

"Forget it. Why don't you just try flying solo for awhile?"

Tena was glad that her sister couldn't see her tears, "I guess…"

"Hey," Kay sliced in, vigorously picking up the pace of her voice, "you don't have to make excuses, or explain a thing to me about men. Jake and I have been married a long time, but I do vaguely recall kissing a couple of toads myself before I found my prince. Speaking of the prince, Jake is running in and out of the door giving me the ice-cream signal. I'm going to hang up now so that you can give Ma a call."

"You're going for ice cream in the middle of this kind of storm? I don't even have electricity here yet."

"You don't? Well, a hurricane wouldn't keep Jake from a Vanilla Twist at the Dairy Bar. Why don't we pick you up?"

"Thanks, but no thanks. As soon as the power is on again, I'm just calling Mom, and then I'm going to take a shower and curl up with my thoughts. I think I just need some time by myself. I want to write down as much as I can remember of this wild story while it's all fresh in my mind."

"Okay, do whatever you need to do," Kay responded with unusual gentleness.

Tena was glad she backed off. She sure wasn't in the mood for ice cream, and didn't think that tonight she could take hearing her brother-in-law's rendition of the Mickey Mouse Club song, or any recounting of their escapades on sunny, sandy beeches.

Kay said, "So, I'll see you at Ma and Ott's on Thursday?"

"Most likely."

"Well then, okay, remember I love ya."

"Love you too."

She had just hung up the receiver when the lights came back on. She called her mother right away, and as she had suspected, her mother had forgotten much of their previous conversation about the North Creek day trip.

Sunday morning after church, Tena went to her mother and Otto's for breakfast. Later, as usual, Otto went off to hit a few balls at the Golf Plantation, obviously glad to leave his wife and her daughter alone for a bit of afternoon girl talk.

"Don't forget we have to be at the fire hall later on. We're signed up for duty at the snack table for the 3:30 shift. It's the annual carnival, remember?" Bertha reminded Otto as he pulled his golf cart past them.

"I remember, dear. I'll be back in plenty of time to hold down the fort."

The women had already begun to toss around gift ideas for an upcoming going away party for Buddy, but as soon as Otto shut the back door behind himself, Tena began to relate the unsettling events of the previous day. She blurted out everything as gently as she could, and it wasn't long before she could tell from her mother's sober expression that every word Tess Waldron had told her was the truth. All she needed was her mother's verbal affirmation.

"I'm surprised that woman is still living," Bertha said. "She sure is a marvel!"

"She told me to say hello, made me promise to come back, and insisted that I bring you along some day."

Bertha shrugged. "Maybe I'll do that... some day. I remember her as very gracious and accepting of me. But, I'm not sure how I would feel about seeing her again. You know, Tena, so much water has gone under the bridge, and I don't know if Otto would approve."

"I guess I might feel the same way if I was in his shoes."

"But, who knows. If this is the same person I am remembering, it must be difficult for a woman like that to end up confined in the old age home."

"Garnet Manor is a beautiful place and anyone can see that the attendants give the residents good care, Mom. She doesn't seem to mind being there. Although she's in a wheelchair, she was very chipper. But, I was wondering about something she said."

"I can imagine that you wondered about a lot of things after your visit."

Tena nodded. "Tess told me that after the war she was in England working. I thought that part weird. After all, she would have had to been quite advanced in age to be still working, wouldn't she?"

"Some older folks hold up pretty good, you know."

"I know, Mom."

"I only met your father's Aunt Tess a couple of times, but he said that she was considered quite a family icon, always going off someplace. She lost her husband early in life and stayed a single, professional woman thereafter. Ben told me that she even wrote a book about her travels. I think she was in Africa long before England. I must admit though, that I still can't get over that she is still with us."

"Africa?"

"That's what I heard." Bertha smiled. "She was a globetrotter. That kind of person goes until they drop."

"So, what Tess says is true?"

Bertha sighed, replying slowly, "Yes, the past comes back to haunt us all, I suppose. Tess was right. Your father was married before. He married his high school sweetheart, but the marriage was terribly unhappy, the way I got it. He told me that she was unfaithful and broke his heart. He said that he had come home from the War, and she was living there at their flat with another man. It was too much for him to take. There was a terrible scene, and he threw the guy down a flight of stairs. Still, your father loved her, and she asked for forgiveness, so he stayed a couple of months, before he awoke one morning and she was gone. I always thought that was when he took up the drink."

"You knew? I can't believe that you never told me or... Kay."

"I asked Kay not to say anything about your father having been married. Kay was just doing as I had asked, and so you can't hold it against her that she respected my wishes. Truthfully, we didn't know much about his life before I married him. And, after your father died, and I married Otto, I didn't want to resurrect old wounds."

"His first wife's name was Ava," Tena said. "Did you know that?"

"Was it?" Bertha responded stiffly. "Yes, I knew of her. I knew about the little boy too. In fact, you were a toddler when your father had a letter from her saying how he was to be adopted by her new husband, and that's when Ben told me about the boy. I was startled and hurt that he would keep such a thing from me, but I got over it. I was so in love with him. It hurt less not to think about what happened in his past."

Tena took hold of her mother's hand. "I can see this is painful for you to talk about, but I have to know. Please try to understand."

"I understand more than you give me credit for Tena. From what I could surmise, your father didn't want anything to do with Ava after their divorce, and I imagine that Ava felt likewise. He told me that he had not seen his son since he was an infant, and always questioned if the child was his own. So, when his first wife wanted him to sign papers giving up all rights to the little boy, your father did so."

"What an awful mess that all must have been," Tena said. "Can you believe she had brought this boy; his name is Johnny, to see Tess. Tess insists he's a Waldron."

"No kidding. I always suspected that his wife was pregnant when Ben came home from the service. I used to think that she just wanted to keep face, which was probably why she stayed with him that few months. But as the years have passed I thought to myself that maybe I wanted it to be that way. It was easier for me to think of her as a cheat, than to think that the man you love would give up his own flesh and blood."

"All I can say is that Tess really believes he is a Waldron."

"He could be Ben's child; only God knows that truth. But if Ben was the father, then this Johnny is your half-brother."

Tena scraped the remainder of her uneaten scrambled eggs into the garbage. "That's kind of hard for me to take in just now. Think of this, Mom; he's not a child anymore, and I learned that he's been up recently to see Tess Waldron."

Bertha appeared startled, "My goodness, that is a coincidence: him deciding to do such a thing just when you did."

"Isn't it?" Tena whispered.

Bertha said, "I never said anything to Kay about this, but several years after your father died, I received a copy of a letter from his brother. He wrote to me through a Mr. Brian who was the coroner at the time of your father's death and had become a prominent attorney in Albany back in those days. It just so happened that Mr. Brian's brother owned Carlton Insurance where I worked as a receptionist for a few years. Your uncle wanted me to know that Ava and her husband were living just a few miles away in Lansingburgh. She must have written to him for some reason or another, and he must have had sudden pangs of guilt for ignoring you. I remember being so mad about his letter, because he hadn't bothered with us for so many years, but had obviously kept tabs on them. I was so disgusted that I had no desire to write back to him, and so I never found out how on earth he knew that he could get in touch with me by way of Mr. Brian. Later, when Ava and her husband were killed in that awful pileup on Route 4, I read about it in the paper and recognized the name."

"Good grief!" Tena said, running her hands through her hair.

Absently, Bertha drew a glass of water from the faucet placing it on the counter. She stood staring out the window over the sink. "God forgive me, it is an awful thing to say, but I thought their deaths had brought closure to that part of my life. Somehow I had foolishly forgotten that God chooses the time and place for everything. Just like it seems now is the time that He has decided for you to know all about the past. I can't do anything about what happened, but I can't help wishing. To be honest, I wish that so many things could have been different in my life, but who are we to question God's direction of our lives? Anyhow, now you can see why I would be reluctant to visit Ben's aunt."

Tena sank into a kitchen chair. "This is all a huge surprise, but you know the most colossal revelation of all is that I thought you told Kay everything. I've always had it in my mind. Listen, I don't hold it against Kay that she would keep your secrets. If you had asked me not to say anything, I would have done the same."

"I think some secrets are better left alone, Precious, but had I believed that child was your brother, I would have told you all about this long ago. I see now I was wrong."

"I'm sorry you're upset, Mom, but I'm not sorry that all this is out in the open."

"Don't worry about my feelings. Strangely enough, I'm more relieved than upset. I always wanted to tell you more about your father, but I had reservations. Despite how everything ended up with your father and me, we were happy at one time. He was handsome and very bright. I know I've never told you this either, but he was quite a singer."

"He liked music?"

"He did indeed, and he enjoyed singing along with the radio to me."

"That was nice, Mom."

Bertha nodded. "Yes, it was. I do have some good memories. We married promising each other we'd make a fresh start. In the beginning, I felt we were doing just that. Of course, I knew he drank socially on occasion, but I had no idea that he was an alcoholic. I have come to know that stuff is poison.

"After our second year together his drinking had increased, but by then you were born, and I truly believed that I could help him. For a while he acted as though he wanted my help. He went to his AA meetings faithfully. For a time the program seemed to work for him. I don't know what happened. What can I say? He started drinking again, and became abusive. I don't know why. I wish I had the answers."

"Maybe it was her that did it to him," Tena commented flatly. "Here he was, out there fighting a war, and she was shacking up with another guy. Can you imagine what that had to do to him?"

"Yes, I'm sure that it was terrible. I would imagine that such a thing left him with a deep scar, but don't forget, that was in the past when he and I married. I wouldn't want to diminish the good that was in your father, but he failed me and he failed you. He accepted the blame for all of that in the end. He let me know that he did in a note before he died."

"I think I'm beginning to understand," Tena said softy.

"Good."

"Mom, what do you know about the 'heavenly farm'?" The way Tess told the story, it seems that my father and his brother should have inherited money from the sale of that property. Unless I misunderstood her, that farm was sold to the resort people."

"I told you before; I don't know anything about any property up there. Certainly, I never saw any money, and I never heard your father speak about selling any land. If that had happened it must have been years before we met. Don't forget he had been away from North Creek for quite awhile by then."

"You can't remember anything at all?"

Bertha started to laugh. "We lived in a coldwater flat on what he made from the railroad. I am sure that if your father had a large inheritance we would have moved to a nicer neighborhood. As for the rest, I never knew that he grew up on a farm. He told me that his father was a carpenter."

"Tess may have mentioned that my grandfather was a carpenter. You could still own a farm and be a carpenter as well."

"That's true," Bertha replied.

"Maybe there wasn't much money from the sale, but goodness, it was over two hundred acres and a house. You would think that there would have been something."

Bertha's laughter slipped away. "After I left your father, I went back to work in the factory, and there were times when I didn't know where our next meal was coming from. Thank God that Kay and my family helped us through. After all, I only made thirty eight dollars a week when I was working at Baby Togs. One year, before I went to work for the insurance company, things were so tight that I took an extra Saturday morning job cleaning offices downtown just to make ends meet. I can assure you that there is no pot of gold at the end of any rainbow, if that's what you're thinking. I saw what was in that flat he had back then after he died. Believe me; he wasn't living in the lap of luxury. If he ever had any inheritance he must have drunk it all away."

"Guess my imagination is working overtime."

"I think it may be."

"Just the same, I've decided to take my vacation up there. I'm going to rent a hotel room and stay for a week. There's just so much more I'd like to know."

"Will Cindy's husband allow her to go with you?

Tena giggled. "Dave won't have to give his approval. Cindy isn't going with me. I'm going by myself."

"Oh, Tena, a woman all by herself on a long road trip could have such problems. What if your car breaks down on one of those desolate country roads? I don't know if vacationing up there all by yourself is such a good idea."

"I'll be fine. You have to stop worrying about me all of the time. I'm a big girl now."

"I don't know about that."

"When I get there I'll call you every night. Would that make you feel better?"

Bertha looked at the floor. Dubiously she replied, "Somewhat."

"Then I'll call and make the reservation. I'll keep you posted by phone every step of the way."

Bertha nodded. "You're the stubborn one, you always have been, and so if you're determined to go I suppose keeping me informed is the best I can ask. Other than this trip, what else is going on with you, Dovey? You broke off with Ken, didn't you?"

"Ken and I are finished, Mom. I told Kay the same."

"You seem to be all right about it. Are you?"

"Yes, I will be."

"I'm sorry it didn't work out for you two kids, but of course, that is the wisdom in a long courtship."

"You know, Mom, I don't want to talk about Ken. I'm looking forward to other things now."

"Okay, I won't ask about him anymore, but if you want to talk anytime, you just come over and we will."

Tena nodded, finishing up the remainder of the breakfast plates; she placed the last into the dish rack to drain. "I don't know, it all seems surreal to me."

"Going back to the possibility that this young man is your half-brother, I must say that I find it very peculiar that you seem to be introduced to two mysteries at the same time."

"Two mysteries?"

"You know, the spoon and then this other. I've racked my brain about that little spoon. Just seems strange; such a coincidence."

"Sure does."

"And another thing has just struck me. If your father's family owned a farm of any size, Ava would have known about the place. If her son is suddenly snooping around after all of these years, there must be a reason," Bertha said, picking up her embroidery hoop.

"Did you ever wonder, Mom, why my father's brother, Bob, went out west and never came back? I mean, if the Waldrons had such deep roots in North Creek, why would Bob never return to New York? Why would anyone leave home and hardly ever come back to visit?"

Tediously separating strands of violet thread, Bertha replied, "Who knows? It seems strange to you and me because we're a close knit family, but, it isn't so unusual for some people. Bob did come back for the funeral, and he did pay for Ben's headstone, I give him credit for that, but as far as I ever knew that was the last time he came east. Although he could have been buried in the family plot up there in the Union Cemetery next to his brother and their mother and father, he isn't."

"You always said that you didn't believe in visiting graves. I'm surprised that you've been up to the Union Cemetery. You don't drive. Did Ott take you up there?"

"No. During those early years I did visit your father's gravesite on Memorial Day. Matt and Betty Rettinger drove me up, and you heard me right; visiting a grave in my opinion isn't important. You can pray anyplace for one's immortal soul."

"Yes, that's true. Well, I was just wondering."

"Between you and me, the few times that I met your uncle, my impression of Bob was that he was kind of a cold fish. I had the feeling he looked down on your father. Maybe he saw him as weak, what with the divorce and the drinking."

Tena shrugged. "It could be that's why my father never talked much about him to you. It's hard for me to understand. If I lived on the other side of the globe, I'm sure Kay and I would have mortgage-worthy phone bills. I could never just walk away like that."

Bertha smiled contentedly as she continued to root around for the right thread in her sewing basket. "You know, Tena, I'm not blind, I can see that you are still looking for something in the nature of a big discovery up north, and although I'll admit that someone sending you that spoon out of nowhere sure is a mystery, it is very possible, Dear, that everything could be just the way it appears. Maybe the spoon has nothing to do with your father or any of the Waldrons."

Tena raised an eyebrow. "You think that's how it is?"

Bertha looked up from her needlework to meet her daughter's gaze. "Just watch out for yourself when you get up there. Promise me that you will do that much and that you will keep your word and call."

"I promise."

Chapter 6

Tena was beginning to believe that Cindy possessed far more insight into the future than either of them could have imagined. The trophy sitting on her new coffee table had indeed been a catalyst for change. Her freshly altered lifestyle was definitely sandwiched between layers of a barrage of questions, and astonishingly enough, very few of them pertained to her and Ken. She had given up living on Pepto-Bismol.

Still, right now, facing the heart of the summer advertising season, all questions about her personal life had to be put on a back burner as the Record braced for the Fourth of July publicity campaign. Who remembered any of the rules learned in June's stress management class, as they scurried around from customer to customer, blending in special holiday ads with the regulars, and pushing up deadlines to accommodate the bulk. Every retailer in town demanded best placement in the paper's special edition for America's Bicentennial Anniversary. The ads with the expensive red, white, and blue splashes of color had put them in the black. Management was happy. Patriotism paid!

Tena tossed her layouts onto the top composing room shelf. Her head pounded. At 10 A.M. she had been on the brink of complete disaster, but she struck a goldmine at 10: 15 when one of her key accounts called begging to get one, last minute, very special, quarter page ad into print. She had flown out of the office, racing back, barely making the twelve o'clock deadline. Exhausted, dragging herself out of the building, she scolded herself for the umpteenth time for not being brave enough to open up that dress shop last year with her cousin, Nancy.

Where was all the glamour promised in her interview four years ago? For that matter, where was she going? Was this it? There had to be something more to life than grinding away at a job, having kids, and ending up in a grave that nobody – including the children you'd given a life to – visited. Sure, there were those magic career moments, but primarily the job was monotonously demanding. She suddenly realized that her mom told a lot less half-truths than she did. She told them to Cindy and again when insisting to her mother that she liked her job. Despite the fleeting high provided by the Diamond Award, enthusiasm for the routine of shuffling ads had become increasingly a bore. How many ways could one sell cars, or recliners, or juicy ripe tomatoes? How many times could she do a bang-up gangbuster ad selling a plaid couch?

Among fourteen grumbling salespeople suffering from acute insomnia and migraines, Tena, as the team lead, regularly searched for the promised fun that would sustain them all from pay check to pay check. Fortunately, although she was no longer crazy for the job, God had blessed her with stalwart comrades in arms. On many occasions they would all put their heads together, and before long ideas would be jumping together like grasshoppers. Salvation was this amusing bunch of mixed personalities who could invariably cipher out the hilarity from the humdrum, a squad in which each had found their present calling in unusual ways.

Ruth, forty-three, divorced, and a former pediatric nurse, a double path that Ruth insisted had prepared her exceptionally well for the advertising business, was a proud new grandmother with a wallet full of snapshots.

Ed, an African-American, who handled the west end territory where the key accounts were all sports clubs, walked with a permanent limp. Ed didn't volunteer details on his personal life, but did threaten to quit every other day. He, nor anyone else, ever mentioned a wife or kids, so it was assumed that he was single. Rumor was that he had been in 'Nam, and his limp was from a gunshot wound. The only personal information about him that anybody was truly privy to was in knowing that at precisely 6:30 every Wednesday evening you could find him at the Nesting Bar and Restaurant on Tenth Street. He swore that his one reason for being there was to jot down the menu specials for the upcoming weekend ads. Nobody believed him.

Harry had taught high school math for ten years in the Bronx. One afternoon after a drug shootout, Harry came home from work to find the outline of the body of one of his students in his driveway. He, his wife, and their six children moved upstate in the early seventies, and thereafter he never taught again. He handled major department stores and national account co-op advertising.

Then there was Buzz Newland who graduated from the Pratt School of Art. Buzz spent more time in the composing room than out selling. Most nights he joined Jack Breen from Editorial after work at the Beaverwyck Lounge in Rensselaer.

It always fascinated Tena that except for herself, none of these people on the "sales team" had a lick of selling experience prior to day-one working for the newspaper. She had sold cosmetics at Macy's during college, and guessed that for this reason, the Record's Advertising Director, Mike Herald, had hired her. She remembered applying for the position at the paper. She wasn't sure she'd be able to sell advertising, but during a second interview Mike discovered that besides various moisturizers, mascara, and eyeliner, she had also sold over three thousand lipsticks during her two year stint at the store. That night Mike's assistant had called her mother's house to offer her the job.

Three weeks into the job, after what would be the first of many selling defeats, Mike glibly spouted, "Listen, kid, don't worry about a thing, if you can sell lipsticks, you can sell ads. It's all war paint."

Work this morning had begun the usual way: each of them bumping into one another at the swing door to the composing room that never stopped swinging, and each of them mumbling complaints about inconsiderate clients. Passing Ruth's desk she was surprised when Ruth asked her how her trip north had gone, casually mentioning that her cousin's mother-in-law was a new resident up at Garnet Hill home. "My former hubby's family is from up there, you know," Ruth volunteered. With yesterday's paper in hand, Tena glanced at her uncomprehendingly while flipping to the Entertainment section. In truth she had only half heard what Ruthie was talking about. "Damn, damn, damn!"

"What? What's the matter?"

"They've got the wrong menu in again for Harry's Beef Place. The special is supposed to be fish, not chicken. Fish is tonight. It says Friday fish night and they stick in Thursday's special. Oh God, Harry is going to spit nails at me. I can hear him now...."

"Yup, so can I," Ruth sighed. "His favorite old song, 'I'm not paying for that ad.'"

Livid, Tena turned back toward composing, but Clem Tollman, her Retail Manager, grabbed her by the arm, stopping her by the door.

"Whatever it is, it can wait. Congratulations. Your squad is up eighteen percent," he said, rocking back on his heels. "Hip Hip, it's bonus time!"

Ruth rolled her eyes and wandered off.

"Thanks, Clem, I'm thrilled beyond words, but besides Ruth and me, did you pass along the praise and glory to the rest of my people?"

"I did, you know," Clem barked as he disappeared down the hall grinning ear to ear.

Good, Tena thought. Hitting a home run was a great way to close up shop on a Friday before going on a vacation, especially since Clem had promised each of them a small bonus if they exceeded their goal. They had done that, it appeared, and then some. So, for today, everybody was a happy winner, and they would be able to stay ahead of the creditors for another two weeks. But once again the intangible highs spurred on by professional success would be short lived and best savored quickly. Next week it would be, *so what have you done for me lately?* After vacation she knew that she'd be back at square one again, calling out signals, waving her pom-poms, and kissin' up to foulmouthed Harry, but for now she was ahead in this campaign and could leave with a good feeling in her stomach.

When five o'clock came she raced like a panther for her car. All she could think about was her reservation for a week's stay at the Pine Cone Inn, a short jump outside of North Creek. From the brochure the place looked to be a charming quiet country inn. As she read the pamphlet again she decided that the inn's publicity person did a great job of painting up the amenities with color photos of a new in-ground pool and full country breakfast each morning. She also liked the references to local Lake George attractions and the history of the Pine Cone. Eighteen dollars a night was more than reasonable.

As for Ken, she hadn't heard from him all week. She was surprised how little she had thought about him. Maybe Kay was right. Broken hearts did heal.

Chapter 7

Saturday, before checking into the Pine Cone Inn, Tena had another destination. She felt it important to try to find the cemetery where her father was buried. How could she begin such a journey into the past without first demonstrating some sign of respect? He had been a veteran, so she had purchased a wreath of artificial red, white and blue flowers decorated with tiny American flags.

This time, rather than marking miles with a boring highway drive, she took Aunt Jane's advice and traveled the scenic route toward Sellersville, passing some of the old, Dutch houses along the Glen Kill Creek. It was good to see that a few had been restored, but many of them were shadows of by-gone days, not much more than fieldstone foundations lost among the tall weeds and fallen, broken trees. It was hard to imagine the vast, productive farmlands these earliest grand manor houses had once overlooked. She couldn't help but wonder about the people who had inhabited them.

Sunlight glared against the windshield when two, young, whitetail deer leapt from the thick roadside brush. Tena slammed on the brake pedal, barely missing them, forcing her car to the side of the two-lane road. Once safely across the road the pair paused in the field, their tails flickering nervously. *Close call, right, buddies?*

Shaking, she took a deep breath, looked up, and noticed the sign for Bossardville Junction, "population 513". It was as if the deer were sent to point her in the right direction.

Her mother had said the Union Cemetery where her father was buried was somewhere after the town of Bossardville and was positioned on a hillside along the road before you entered North Creek. Or had she said north of the two towns? At this point, Tena couldn't remember what her mother's directions had been, but her scoffing and final warning rang in her ears. *Going there is a morbid waste of time. The dead need prayers, not flowers. Don't be standing at my stone weeping over me when I go because I won't be there. God willing, I'll be up in heaven living with the Lord in His beautiful garden. Just keep me in your prayers, and don't waste hard earned money on flowers. Watch out for yourself and call me.*

Back on track after her brush with the deer, she slowly entered the town that, like Troy, although considerably smaller, had once been renowned for its mills producing detachable collars worn by men across the country back in the 1800's. She counted six boarded up abandoned brick factories before cruising past the frontage of Kelly's Bar, and the near empty lot of Peratta's Groceries. After continuing on for what might be about a mile beyond the edge of town, she thought she heard a muffled but insistent voice…*Turn here! Turn in!*

Needing to get her bearings and remembering Grandma Honey's advice not to ignore such prompts that came from within, she spotted an opening to a small gravel drive. She slowed the car to a crawl and parked. Staring down the desolate, lonesome lane that led to an isolated, overgrown meadow, strewn with ancient markers, she tried rolling back the years to childhood and her father's funeral. Could this possibly be the place where her father had been laid to rest? Even though she thought that her mother had said that the Union Cemetery was between Bossardville and North Creek, something told her that this *wasn't Union Cemetery.*

Dubious, she got out of her car and began walking toward perhaps fifty tombstones enclosed within the small graveyard. The sad, unkempt, old stones, many sunken three quarters into the earth, seemed to sing out with one voice. She bent to read an epitaph.

"Hello there," a gentle whisper came from behind. Tena bolted and twirled around facing a short, thin woman dressed in a kaki colored raincoat that was tied snugly mid-center of her waist as if the day were cold and rainy, rather than hot and sticky as was so typical of early July. She appeared to be in her early fifties.

"Dear God, you startled me!"

"I am sorry. I did not mean to frighten you." The woman's soft voice held a unique accent, her eyes full of apology.

"That's okay; I just thought that I was alone. You surprised me."

"Who do you seek?"

"At the moment I'm not seeking anyone in particular. Just getting my bearings, but I'm beginning to think I'm lost," Tena mumbled.

"Lost?"

"I'm not sure I'm where I'm supposed to be," Tena answered.

"It seems we are both drawn here to this beautiful garden of souls."

"I enjoy reading the old inscriptions. Garden of souls is such a lovely way to put it, and this spot is so very peaceful."

The woman nodded her agreement. "My good husband is laid over yonder," she said solemnly, pointing to the far corner of the clearing.

"Oh, I'm sorry," Tena said, observing that the stranger's coat appeared to be wool. She found herself trying to identify her accent.

"No need to be sorry. He is with the Almighty Lord now. Yet, you are indeed kind to speak so. Come," she invited, "you must tell me whom you are seeking."

Tena had walked past stones marked Meyer, Robblee, Richards, Hills, but found no Waldrons while exploring the circumference of the cemetery. "I'm meandering more than seeking," she said. "I'm actually looking for the grave of my father, Ben Waldron, but I've gotten confused. I'm sure I made a wrong turn. My father died in the 1950's, and it's obvious that no one could have been buried in this cemetery for generations. As I said, I'm just rambling around; I have all the time in the world. I'm on vacation and I like reading the old stones."

Listen to me, Tena thought. *I sound like a bumbling idiot. Why do I need to clarify myself to this lady anyway?*

As if reading her mind, the woman assumed a role of tour guide, beckoning her forward. Tena, obedient and silent, followed the placid Pied Piper toward the end of the path near the edge of the woods that met the grassy meadow. She stopped, and they stood together under several massive hemlocks. Right away, Tena's eyes rested upon one cracked slab.

The woman spoke with deliberateness, "This is the final resting place of Garret Waldron who was one of the first settlers in these parts. Come…read for yourself."

Tena leaned toward the inscription. *Garret Waldron, Born May 31, 1738 – Died July 3, 1829. God Keep Him In Thy Holy Grace. I wonder if this could be one of my ancestors,* Tena whispered to herself, and she thought she heard the woman say "A church once was built upon this spot. A tragedy it was when God's sacred house burned to the ground."

"I would imagine that this must have been the churchyard."

"Yes, I come often to this place. It's so peaceful, and I knew many who are here."

Tena was half listening, "Oh, yes, I can see what's left of the building foundation over there," she said pointing to a broken line of moss-covered fieldstones.

"My husband, Adam, and I attended services here."

"Oh? Are any more Waldron's to be found here?" Tena asked while re-examining the irregular rows.

"I assure you, Miss, there are no other Waldrons here, only Garret Waldron. His sons and daughters scattered across the land, but sure am I that you will find whom and what you seek."

"Well, I hope so." Tena answered absently, already kneeling near the old stone again. "It's a shame the marker is so damaged. I'd try to straighten it up, but I'm afraid I'd only make it worse."

"I am sure he would be glad of your kind thought," the woman remarked softly.

Tena laughed nervously. "Gosh, I've got goose bumps all of a sudden. Something seems kind of odd…"

"What does, Miss?"

"I wonder why Garret is the only Waldron here?" Tena said, rubbing her arms. Clouds had begun to gather, and the sun had disappeared. She was actually beginning to feel chilly.

"I should think so, Miss, but there are no more. Now, you will forgive me, but I must go to be by my husband."

"Oh, yes, of course, Tena mumbled, staring at the epitaph. She didn't get up. An eerie feeling ran through her as she suddenly realized that the date of Garret Waldron's death, well over one hundred years ago, was the same as today, July 3rd. More determined than ever to read the rest of the inscription at the bottom of the sunken stone, her face now nearly touched the earth. Finally, she pieced together the first line of the eroded words... ***Thy hand rests upon thee...***

Obviously there was more, but the remainder of the intended thought was buried in the ground, a victim of the finger of time. She rose from her knees, brushing away the dirt from her jeans. Coming back to the present she scanned the cemetery for her new acquaintance that had respected her solitude and no doubt went to pray and seek comfort beside the grave of her dead husband. Strangely, the woman was nowhere in sight.

Tena continued to search for her as she walked back toward her car parked near the road, all the while thinking that she would surely encounter another car nearby to her own. She felt badly that she had not really introduced herself, nor had she said a proper goodbye. In fact, the more she thought about it, the more she realized that she had, in practically ignoring the woman's presence, been unforgivably rude to an obviously lonely soul who had reached out to her.

However, as she approached her vehicle there was no other car in sight, nor were there any tire tracks or other visible signs that another car had been there. The breeze had dissipated; not a bird stirred. She was alone.

Tena couldn't imagine how the woman could have disappeared so quickly. She stood by her car looking up and down the road. Could she have come from a nearby farm? Would she see her later walking home along the roadway?

The day had moved on so quickly. Where had the time gone? It was already after 4:30. She had to get moving. There was no time left to continue looking for the woman or the Union Cemetery. Unbelievably, she had lingered at this cemetery for over an hour. If she continued at this pace she would be late checking into the Pine Cone Inn, and now began to hope that the innkeeper would keep her reservation.

Chapter 8

George and Lillian MacArthur began their life at the Pine Cone Inn in the spring of 1951, the year after they had been married.

During his three years, two months, and fourteen days of military duty, George had often envisioned himself owning a piece of America. His dream had made the long, lonely hours spent in dirty, wet, trench holes overseas bearable. He thought when he got back he didn't have to become a big tycoon, he just wanted his own place.

George was a proud holder of the Bronze Star. When the War was over, he submitted his application for a GI loan, and before long had purchased a small resort hotel in the clear, clean, mountain air that he had grown up in just outside of the town of North Creek, New York. He couldn't believe it. The little inn was the centerpiece of his vision. Finally it had become a beautiful reality.

He soon met the girl of his dreams as well. He figured that there couldn't be another couple on the planet who were as crazy in love as he and his Lil. When George carried his lovely bride, the former Lillian LaRose of Virginia, over the threshold, the New York Adirondacks had once again begun to swell with summertime tourists.

At the turn of the century it had been the trains that carried folks northward to the cool mountain breezes, but soon rigorous advance of the so called "tin-can tourist" had begun.   People by the carload abandoned their muggy, clustered Manhattan apartments for the cool freshness of the high peaks of the northern part of the Empire State.   In addition, twice as many Canadians traveled the short two-hour drive from cosmopolitan Montreal to enjoy the attractions of Lake George village, take in a thoroughbred race at Saratoga's colorful Flat Track during the August season, or enjoy the crystal pure healing waters of that city's famous spa.

Beginning in April, Canadians and New Yorkers alike rushed to fish at Loon or Indian Lake, enthusiasts wading hip deep in the surrounding speckled trout filled streams spilling over timeworn blue-gray boulders.

Thus it continued throughout the summer. However, with the passing of Labor Day, school classes reconvened for the children, and families went home to their city hubs. Familiar haunts like the Pine Cone Inn remained favorites throughout golden autumn for retired kindred souls renewing their hearts.

Brisk mornings in November found the inn filled to capacity once again with deer hunters, while winter brought the carnival on ice, giant ice sculptures, and more fishing from the ice-holes in the center of the shacks on the frozen lakes. Mid-December heralded the lucrative ski season, but parties began in the lodges at the sight of the first flakes.

The seasonal cycle went round and round. Before long, tiny buds appeared on trees, hikers were on the trails, and the sound of oars splashing in Martha's Pond blended with the fluted song of the wood thrush.

George and Lillian had found Jimmy Stewart's 'wonderful life'.

Eventually, Lil MacArthur became somewhat famous in her own right. She had brought more than her genteel southern manners and determined spirit to her new Yankee home. She was a marvelous cook, renowned especially for her delicious Virginia corn pancakes. When pressed for the recipe, she'd tell her neighbors that it was a secret passed down from her grandmother, and she wouldn't dare break a sacred family trust.

During the week, Lillian would cook only for her registered guests, however, on Sundays after church services, she'd open her doors to the general public. They came in droves for her hearty southern breakfast. It wouldn't be uncommon that a guest would have to wait a half hour outside of the inn before being seated. Tables were always at a premium.

Lillian prided herself on her refined, accommodating ways as much as on her culinary skills. She would insist that one of her waitresses tote a pot of coffee to waiting customers and offer a cup to patient patrons while they waited to put pancake to palate. She wouldn't have a surly, unhappy customer come sit at one of her tables to partake in a family food tradition. Whatever would people think?

The Southern lady's considerate practices were appreciated. During the twenty plus years of her and George's proprietorship their eight rooms were seldom empty.

Inn keeping had been a good venture, yet as time went on the childless couple decided that they might like to semi-retire, so to speak. It would be nice to travel to a warmer climate during the winter season. They had both taken up golf in recent years. Golf wasn't easily played in the Adirondack northern snow.

They did consider selling out completely, but decided that they still wanted to retain their northern home as a summertime residence. They'd live part of their time in sunny Florida, away from the bite of the winter winds and the perils of driving in the snow that they had so rejoiced over in their younger years. But, things just weren't working out. One problem or another kept getting in the way. There were constant repairs to be done, and it was difficult to find anyone who wanted the full responsibility of running the inn for several months at a stretch. In addition, business had begun to drop off ever since the new Smithfield resort had been put into service at the base of Whiteface Mountain. It was beginning to look as if they would never get to Florida, but in 1974 something happened that gave George and Lillian renewed hope. Lillian's nephew, Kirk, came to spend time at the Pine Cone after having suffered what appeared to be a nervous breakdown.

His condition was a minor set back, Lillian insisted. She assured her husband that she knew that was all it was because her sister Sarah had written her regularly about Kirk's little health problem. After all, Kirk was very successful. He just needed a break.

The story George and Lillian received was that although financially fattening, chasing the ticker tape on Wall Street had taken its toll on Sarah's boy. Sarah was rather embarrassed that Kirk couldn't stand the pressure of it all anymore. She confided he was having terrible troubles coping, and it was definitely showing on him. She knew this first hand since Kirk had been staying with her and Will for the better part of a month.

Because of his breakdown he had been forced to take a leave from his Wall Street position. Lord knew when he'd be able to go back to all of that, but Sarah wondered if Lillian and George wouldn't mind taking their nephew in as a border for a few weeks while he got his stamina back. She thought that if her son were able to relax in the Adirondack countryside far away from the stressful demands of the city, he would be able to collect himself and come to some decision as to his future.

George considered all of his sister-in-law's maternal ramblings a bunch of who-ha. It appeared to him that she had always pampered her eldest boy far too much, and although Lillian didn't want to hear it, he sensed that Kirks "trouble" had nothing to do with work. More likely, his difficulties had all to do with a woman. A dozen years before as a high school senior he had impregnated a seventeen-year-old classmate. She and her family had suddenly departed for California for "family reasons." And there had been rumors about other "accidents" for years after that.

The result of Kirk's lack of restraint sometimes gave George pause to wonder what the good Lord had in mind when dispensing His miracle of life. Here were he and Lil praying daily, and for years doing their damndest to be blessed with a child, while Kirk and his lady friends who carelessly played at lust and love were leaving a trail of unwanted babies strewn behind.

"Kirk didn't do right by that girl," He remembered complaining to his wife.

"He couldn't have done anything at all," Lillian protested "when the family left Virginia practically in the middle of the night. Nobody had the opportunity."

George didn't think it best to probe deeply into his wife's family's problems, yet it sure did irk him that not a soul ever knew what had happened to that girl or the child, nor did anyone attempt to find out. He wondered how Lil's sister and her husband could live with themselves knowing that flesh of their flesh was unaccounted for someplace in California. But then, George knew that there were some wrongs in this life that just could never be made right.

After college graduation, Kirk joined his family's bustling real estate business, and shortly thereafter he became engaged to a lovely young woman by the name of Sally LeVern. Lillian had insisted that she and George travel south to show their family support by attending the young couple's engagement party, and so they did, but it was clear that Kirk didn't plan to stick with any of these arrangements. There never was a marriage; within a year a letter arrived from his mother saying how he had moved north to Manhattan. The only thing that Kirk had taken along was his degree in Marketing. He had found a very good position with a New York brokerage house, and his mother bragged how he was living the good life in a swanky apartment on the Upper West Side. George wasn't surprised.

Of course, at first Kirk's father was dumbfounded as well as furious that his son had left them and his fiancee cold on the spot without concerning himself with explanations. It was extremely embarrassing. They had forgiven him for "messing up" when he was a kid, but now he was a young man. But Kirk's dad wasn't angry for long after the stock dividends came in on the investments made for him.

Then the letter arrived for Lillian where Sarah gushed over her son's courtship with his well-connected boss's very beautiful daughter. George and Lillian had not actually met this young lady, but Kirk had sent her picture. Her photograph showed that she was indeed a beauty. Once again, Lillian enthusiastically made arrangements with her nephew to meet them both, this time during the holidays, but she came down with a mild case of the flu and was unable to go. Later, disillusioned yet unwavering in her loyalty, she admitted that it was just as well that she had stayed home when six months later Kirk was unemployed and back home in Virginia. At the time, George's heart went soft when he saw his wife weeping in the kitchen over her morning coffee, a letter in her hand. George figured that something went sour with Lillian's beloved nephew, but he refrained from inquiring about it. A week later Lillian told him about Kirk's breakdown, and she asked if they could put him up for awhile. George stewed about it for a day or so mainly because of Kirk's troublesome ways, but then relented.

The very first day that his nephew arrived at the Pine Cone Inn, George took him aside and laid down the law. As politely as he could put it, he told Kirk to keep his hands in his pockets and away from the girls.

Kirk feigned a pretense of insult, but he understood precisely his uncle's meaning. He assured George that whatever interaction occurred between him and the ladies of the area, he would conduct himself with the utmost gentlemanly dignity.

Temporarily satisfied, George decided to let it go for Lillian's sake, but their new border wouldn't be getting a free ride. No sir! He would have to work for his keep.

The second day after his arrival Kirk was put at the front desk manning the telephone and taking reservations. To George's astonishment, Lillian's irresponsible nephew showed his ardor for business by diving headfirst into his assigned duties. Within a short time Kirk asked if he couldn't try out a few of his own ideas about running the place, implying that George and Lillian were a little bit "old-fashioned". That night, when George crawled into bed with his wife, he admitted that Kirk had pleasantly surprised him a whole lot, but thought that he was a bit presumptuous at times.

Lillian sighed and asked that he just give the boy a chance.

"That's what I'm doing, Dear," he purred as he turned over and closed his eyes.

George's second surprise was his discovery that Kirk's ideas had panned out, especially his early evening tea and sherry hour. Every afternoon from 4 to 6, free tea, coffee, sherry, and hors d'oeuvres were laid out in the parlor. Guests would mingle and get acquainted leading to a much more convivial setting. After a few months, word had spread of the wonderful atmosphere at the old Pine Cone, and bookings were up twenty percent to nearly full capacity. Florida might well be a possibility after all.

No one actually knew when the part ownership notion was conceived, but it was unanimously agreed by the MacArthurs that almost immediately after arriving at the Pine Cone, Kirk had become their right hand man.

So, Kirk's temporary reprieve took a permanent, unexpected turn as he agreed to a six-month management apprenticeship. He would bring new ideas to the table and George would consider his suggestions.

This arrangement went far better than George and his wife anticipated. Kirk's business degree and experience in the Big Apple accorded them an astute marketer. Neither he, nor Kirk, ever mentioned their first day chat on the moralities of life, and Lillian glowed when listening to George tell her sister over the telephone of how impressed he was with all Kirk's help.

Within the year Kirk had invested his savings into the Pine Cone Inn, putting him well on the road to a full partnership. His monetary investment opened the door to big changes at the inn.

The country's Bicentennial was just around the corner, a convenient marketing tool that Kirk had suggested long before the ball dropped at Times Square. Soon crews were working round the clock renovating the entire lodge in Red, White and Blue. Kirk ordered the largest American flag that Lillian had ever seen in her life, and then hung it from the second floor porch rail.

Their biggest expenditure, however, was the grand, in-ground, twenty by fifty foot, concrete swimming pool, the bottom inlaid with five thousand bright mosaics depicting the American Flag. Kirk had the pool set in just a few feet away from the flagstone patio that George had lovingly built with his own hands as a gift for his wife when they had celebrated their twentieth anniversary. The chaise lounges were also given a fresh look with new pads covered with splashy red, white and blue flowers.

George had begun experiencing chest pains when Lillian teamed up with her nephew and he began writing checks to cover their vision of the new Pine Cone. "Deco Power" Kirk called it, and Lillian's lips curved toward the heavens. Soon there were gold American eagles flying resplendently against white satin wall coverings in her "Lobby", previously called the entrance hall.

"Gorgeous," Lillian suggested thoughtfully "now maybe we'll draw a better clientele. Those metropolitan New York people won't stick a toe in the lake. You know how they are,

George. Big city people are far more discriminating about those things than the trout fishermen. They want more options, and I do believe that it is our duty to fulfill those needs."

"Nothin' wrong with the trout fishermen. They pay their bills," George had grumbled sullenly.

"Right! You are so on target with all of this, Aunt Lil," Kirk had chimed in, ignoring his uncle. "I myself hate those slimy, fishy things wriggling all around me, and a body just doesn't know what kind of bottom feeding creature might be nipping at your toes in that lake."

"And I'm sure that some of our guests will love not walking way down to the lake."

"I suppose," George conceded.

The old wicker chairs were sent to Goodwill and replaced with Queen Ann style royal blue, cushioned "thrones", or so George called his wife's new porch seating. The only piece of furniture that George insisted that they keep was their old walnut registration desk. Lillian agreed, saying that it lent character.

In the fall of 1975, the day before their RV pulled out of the drive destined for Florida, Lillian planted an abundance of red and white tulip bulbs, confident that when she and George returned in early spring they would be gloriously welcomed.

The renovations pretty much cleaned out the savings account, but George secretly liked the idea of showing his patriotism. And Lillian was delighted with her new pool. She had taken to holding poolside bridge club every Thursday afternoon. What could George say? He never could refuse his wife anything she wanted.

The place did need a sprucing up, but George hated to think what his father, God rest his soul, would have thought of that flag float bobbing around in the swimming pool.

Kirk didn't stop with the furnishings. Being that all this activity was instigated by the Bicentennial, he continuously strove to find innovative marketing ideas that would coincide with the full twelve months of celebrating America's heritage. To this end he listened attentively to George's dinnertime stories about the inn's history, and was especially attentive when George mentioned that when he purchased the property he had researched the land back to 1774, and there had been evidence of a fur trading shack on the site where the inn now stood. The new partner guaranteed his Aunt that they would put their special piece of Americana on the map of prosperity.

Lillian had laughed, but her deep blue eyes sparkled when she nodded her agreement.

"You know, Kirk, there is just no denying that you possess my Grandfather Charlie's charm. I declare, ladies who I haven't seen in years are coming to call. I don't think they are really all that interested in me, or my corn cakes."

Lillian couldn't blame them for wanting to be in Kirk's company. What red-blooded American girl could resist stealing a glance at a six-foot-two, healthy young man with shoulders like Michelangelo's "David"? Lillian also often commented how she loved to hear Kirk's voice. His unique southern diction brought back memories of sweet Virginia, a comment that somehow made George feel unappreciated and a bit concerned.

George pondered his wife's observations. It was true that Kirk appeared completely recovered from the melancholy which had gripped him in New York City, and it was obvious that he was filled with a magnetism that seemed to allure nearly every female he encountered. At thirty he possessed the suave mannerisms of a far more mature man, speaking with a quite exaggerated drawl that mesmerized the northern ladies. David's shoulders, however, might be a stretch of the imagination.

All in all, George was happy with how things were going for them at the inn, but there was always something about Kirk that made him uneasy. He just couldn't put his finger on it.

Kirk kept his part in his and George's secret bargain. He would flatter the women from eighteen to eighty all alike, but he never stepped over the line with any of them, leastwise not that George knew of, and certainly not under the Pine Cone roof. Every one of the ladies he encountered went home from her visit to the inn joyfully believing that Kirk's buttery compliments were gospel truths, and the rosy words spoken were meant only for her. Kirk's mellow, almond eyes conveyed implied intimacies meant to compliment only her.

Sometimes George found their swooning response to Kirk's persona both ridiculous and hilarious. Often he felt it necessary to leave the room before he gave away his true feelings by a facial expression or outright laugh. On occasion he was equally amused by the reaction of the local men to Kirk's debonair behavior when some husbands didn't find their wives enchantment with the Pine Cone's "Dapper Dan" as easy a dish to swallow as Lil's pancakes.

George decided though that it was all innocent enough. His young manager had every Monday and Thursday off, and usually on those days Kirk would take off for parts unknown to him or his wife. George understood a single young man's need to get away from the scrutiny of his elder relatives. He respected that Kirk's personal time be his own. As far as he knew, he hadn't bothered any of the local girls. It was clear that he wanted to stay on George's good side. He stopped loosing sleep over Kirk.

This Saturday afternoon, while humming *America the Beautiful*, George had no regrets as he stood on the top rung of his sixteen-foot stepladder cleaning the hanging, antique brass, mermaid chandelier Lillian recently had installed in the inn's lobby.

The mahogany grandfather clock in the hall struck five times as the front door swung open. His one last unaccounted for reservation had arrived, nearly knocking him off balance as she entered.

"Oh, no! I'm sorry," Tena said, dropping her bags at her side. She reached to steady the ladder as the mermaid swayed ominously over George.

The fixture secured, George began to descend the ladder steps. "It's ok, Miss. I shouldn't have been in the doorway when we're still expecting guests."

"Need any help, George?" Kirk, nearby at the desk, asked with obvious concern. One eye was on the priceless ceiling fixture, the other took note of the willowy young woman with a head of impetuous, long, red hair running down her back like liquid copper.

"No, thanks. I'm about finished in here, but thanks for the offer."

Tena dragged her bulging suitcase across the floor to the base of the reception desk. "I apologize for my late check in."

George folded up his ladder and braced it against the wall. "No problem; glad to have you, Miss." As he looked closer at his newly arrived guest, his chest tightened. He had known only one other with hair that unique color.

Tena felt uncomfortable. Darn her crazy dalliance. She was sure that her reservation must have been given away. "I know I should have checked in over an hour ago," she said nervously. "I got sidetracked with something on the outskirts of town."

Kirk observed George curiously. He seemed to be staring at the woman. *What was wrong with him?*

George quickly recovered himself. "Not a problem at all. We're glad to have you here, late or not."

Kirk pushed the registration book across the desk toward Tena. "We thought that you might have been tied up in traffic. Did you get caught in the parade?"

"No. I must have missed the parade."

"Don't you give any of that another thought. We are delighted that you have chosen to stay with us," Kirk drawled, handing her the pen. "Just fill out this registration form and we'll get you settled in right away."

George lingered by the desk, trying to discreetly read his young guest's signature upside-down.

"I'll be paying in cash, minus my deposit."

"No need to take care of that now," Kirk assured her.

George, smiling, addressed Tena, "You mind if I ask you something?"

Tena, relieved that she didn't lose her accommodations and wouldn't have to turn around and drive all the way back home tonight, was open to questions. "Ask away."

"Are you any relation to Ben Waldron?"

George's question went through Tena like a fire whistle, but she quickly recovered, recalling Tess mentioning her remarkable resemblance to her father, saying something along the line of how she could have been spit right out of her father's mouth.

"Ben Waldron was my father."

"By God, I knew it! You look just like him!"

"You knew my father? She could barely keep her enthusiasm down.

George suddenly folded his arms protectively. He leaned back on his heels. "I was in the service with your dad in North Africa during the War, but we were friends for quite awhile before then. My family moved from Iowa to New York when I was fifteen, and Ben was my first buddy. We were both in the high school band. We graduated, and then later we enlisted in the army together."

"Oh?" Tena said encouragingly.

"Well, I have to get back to work. We'll talk some other time. Enjoy your stay." George picked up the ladder and headed toward the cellar door.

"That would be nice," Tena called after him, but he was gone.

Kirk voiced his displeasure, "My uncle is usually not so abrupt. Actually, I think he's a bit tired; you'll have to forgive him. It's just that we are all a trifle unsettled around here. We're having a full house for our annual Independence Day dinner. I hope you won't be put off by George's strange behavior and you will come. We serve the meal family style at a special price for registered guests like you. I can assure you that there isn't anyone who doesn't beg for seconds of my Aunt Lillian's cooking."

"The dinner sounds wonderful. Thank you."

Kirk picked up her suitcase. "Is this everything, Miss?"

"Yes."

"Fine, then we'll get you settled."

Tena turned to follow, pausing in front of an impressive, floor to ceiling, gilded framed, oil on canvas portrait of a woman dressed in colonial attire. The paint was crazed and was evidently very old. Tena thought it strange that the subject, although fashionably dressed, wore a necklace that appeared to be a string of corn.

Kirk put down the bag and stood beside her. "She's really something, isn't she?"

"Yes, it's almost as if her eyes follow you. She had such an imposing, almost regal look."

"I suspect that was the artist's intent."

"Who was she?"

"We don't know," Kirk answered thoughtfully. From what I've been told, my Aunt Lillian, that's George's wife, found the painting under a blanket up in the back of the attic."

Tena stared into the dark, pensive eyes. "She looks as if she could be Indian."

"We think that she very well might have been," Kirk replied. "Follow me then? We've got Room 6 all set for you, and you'll have plenty of time to unpack and relax before dinner, since seating is at 6:30. Please come down for our tea and sherry period in the parlor. It began at 4, but goes on until 6. You'll not be disappointed should you decide to join us for either."

"Oh, sorry I'm keeping you."

"That's all right," he said picking up her bag.

"The dinner sounds super," Tena said, dragging herself away from the centuries old gaze. "It all sounds wonderful, and I'm sure I'll enjoy meeting the other guests too."

"Well, then good, we'll see you later."

While Kirk escorted Tena to her room, George hurried anxiously to find his wife. He had something unbelievable and urgent to tell her. Ben Waldron's daughter would be sleeping under their roof tonight.

Chapter 9

Tena followed the back walkway alongside the manicured boxwood hedges toward the pool area. Other than the sound of her orange, rubber flip-flops snapping briskly against the flagstone path, and what she assumed was the distant sound of a maid's squealing utility cart, the place was delectably dead. As she passed a small pond capped generously by flowering, yellow water lilies, her enthusiasm for a peacefully therapeutic solo swim in the inn's pool grew. However, her zeal evaporated as she spotted Kirk, sprawled comfortably on one of his Aunt's vivid lounges.

Discreetly scrutinizing his glistening, lean, bronzed body through the privacy of her tinted sunglasses, she remembered Cindy's prophecy and headed toward a lounge on the opposite side of the pool. *No way, I'm staying clear of this one.* Settling in with her paperback copy of <u>The Deep</u>, purchased yesterday at the bookstore in town, she notched her chair to the upright position, opening to her bookmarked chapter.

"Good morning," Kirk called.

"Oh, good morning, Kirk. I'm sorry I disturbed you."

"No graveyard prowling this morning?"

Tena lowered her sunglasses, openly observing Kirk over the rims, "Isn't Thursday your day off, Kirk? I thought at dinner the other night you said that you liked to put some distance between yourself and this place when you're off. 'Spacing yourself from the natives', I believe you put it."

Kirk smiled charismatically. "Oh, my Lord, did I say that?"

"Well, yes, I'm afraid that you did. And, I'd appreciate it if you would strike the graveyard comment too."

"Ouch! I put my big foot into my mouth that time, didn't I? I must have drunk far more Merlot than I should have. If I said anything else out of line that night, please forgive me, Tena. I didn't mean to be disrespectful, although…"

Tena closed the novel, "Really, Kirk, it's not a big deal. You're forgiven."

"It was only that I remembered that you said you've come to check out your roots," Kirk persisted.

"I guess I shouldn't have been so short with you over nothing. I'm sorry too for being so rude to you. I can see how I'd be viewed as a little bit quirky with all this dead ancestor hunting stuff."

"You mentioned that you work for the newspaper, so I suppose searching out the facts is a part of your job."

"Finding the truth could be construed as a part of what I do, but probably not in the way that you're thinking."

"Excuse me?"

"I'm in advertising, not editorial. Getting to know a business and, of course, the people who run the business is generally helpful in selling products or services. Although not editorial, I like to think of my ad copy as news."

"Oh, I see."

"Probably not, but that's okay too."

"Let me say this much, Tena. Until you came out to our humble patio, you're right; I was inclined to make my usual escape, but your presence has somehow changed my mind. It seems the good Lord above is watching out for me today."

"Sir, why I do believe you have a silver tongue."

"Or shovel? Okay, Okay, I hear you. Can I ask you a straight question?"

"Please."

"Why'd you run away so fast the other night...my drunken foul tongue? We hardly had a chance to finish our conversation, and I wanted to ask what you thought of our festivities."

Tena laughed. "I didn't think you were drunk. Were you drunk? Well, anyway I enjoyed myself."

"You sure don't sound overly impressed. I'm disappointed."

He doesn't give up easily, she thought. "The fireworks you set off over the lake were gorgeous, and you were right about your Aunt Lillian's cooking. Really, I complimented her twice on the strawberry shortcake."

Satisfied, Kirk nestled himself back into his chaise. "What a super day it is today. I think I'll be a lazy boy, enjoy the mountain air, and lull around the pool for awhile."

Tena relaxed. What was she getting herself all worked up over anyway, and she certainly couldn't blame Kirk for enjoying the weather. "I can't believe that it's Thursday already," she whispered half to herself, glancing over at him, but it appeared that Kirk had closed his eyes. She guessed he had gotten her subtle message.

She began thinking about all that had transpired since she had arrived in North Creek. Sunday morning she had attended church, and with the help of the pastor, located her father's grave where she laid the wreath. Her simple gesture of respect had been rewarded with an unexpected gift: a few rows away a young man stood playing the bagpipes –"Erin's Lament." It was a beautiful sentimental tune; a captured moment in time that she was sure she would never forget. The next few days had been taken up with further investigations of her long-lost Waldron family, interspersed with prowling in other old graveyards and historical locations around North Creek and the Lake George area. It had all been fun and occasionally very revealing, but on Wednesday, when she saw the sign up in the window at the bookshop for a hike up Gore Mountain, she was more than ready to abandon ancestral research. Her legs ached from yesterday's excursion, but it was worth it. The views had been spectacular.

She waded through her canvas bag for her Johnson & Johnson Baby Oil. One way or another she had to get some color. Precious vacation time was marching along, and she was still milk white except for her shoulders and her nose. Why did the sun always make a beeline for her nose?

As she liberally applied the oil, she stared curiously at the American flag waving at her from the bottom of the pool.

Kirk had opened his eyes surreptitiously, surveying all of his companion's lissome, softly curved body, beginning with her magnificent fiery mane which she had just tied into a high ponytail with a piece of white satin ribbon, and ending at her peach painted toenails.

What a lovely flower she is, he thought. He prided himself that he had few weaknesses …save one. He loved women, and especially couldn't resist a redhead.

"Hey, Tena, I hope you don't think me too insolent or fresh, but I just want to say that you do look mighty fine in that swimsuit. Aren't you going to try out our pool?"

"Maybe later I will when it warms up, but thanks for the compliment."

"Now I'm encouraged to make another confession. You're not going to get mad if I come straight out and say what's on my mind, are you?

Tena turned, "I value honesty."

"Last Saturday night when we were having what I previously thought was such a nice conversation, I recall you mentioning your delicate skin, and how you always like to sunbathe before the noon hour. On Monday, I was off, and I came out here hopeful that we'd run into one another. Obviously, I was out of luck since you weren't here. I had something I wanted to ask you."

Tena raised a dubious eyebrow. She hadn't thought that they had much of a conversation at all. Maybe he *was* drunk. "Oh?"

Kirk smiled charmingly. "Forgive me, but I enjoyed our conversation very much."

"Did I really mention my delicate...skin?"

"You did...and I can see why you would be concerned."

"Funny, I don't remember, and I was drinking Coke. What was it that you wanted to ask?"

Kirk stood up. His dark brown eyes flashed like two pieces of shimmering coal. "I wanted to ask if I could take you to Lake George for a nice dinner one night this week. I know a great place in the village, and I promise I'll be the perfect gentleman."

"Oh, well, I really don't know Kirk...."

"Come on. Tonight is the last chance I'll have to show you the sights. Tell you what I'm going to do. I'll swim a couple of laps while you think on it. If your answer is yes, I'll be delighted, but if not, no high pressure. I'll bow out gracefully."

Kirk climbed the dive ladder and instantly took full command of the board, every muscle of his body poised, an agile leopard transformed into a strategic gull locked onto its target as he entered the aqua below.

Surfacing, he swam to the edge of the pool. "The water is great; you should definitely try it sometime. So, do I win or lose a date with the fair maiden?"

"Tonight?"

"Tonight is my only night off, and you're scheduled to leave us Saturday."

Tena thought, *I'll bet Mr. Wonderful back home thinks I'm up here pining away for him. What's the harm in a casual dinner date? After all, I promised Cindy that I'd move forward.*

"I'd like to go, Kirk, but I'm afraid that I have other plans for tonight."

Kirk hoisted himself out of the pool. "Unfortunately, that surely is the story of my life."

"It's not what you're thinking. Just this morning I promised that I would visit my elderly great aunt up at Garnet Manor this evening. I can't disappoint her. Thursday is family night, and a special dinner is served to residents and their guests. I'm sure that our little visit will be the highlight of her week."

"Lord knows, I do understand family. I have a carload of cousins back in Virginia, and, of course, Aunt Lillian is my mother's sister."

After a moment of silence he added, "You know, all might not be lost since I'm sure the gents and the ladies up there at

Garnet retire early. We could run down to the village in Lake George later. They have a great band...what do you say?"

"You're pretty persistent, aren't you?"

"I do know when I see a good thing."

Tena laughed. "Okay. I'm sure that dinner with my aunt won't last more than a few hours. I'll go out with you. I like to dance, but I'm giving you fair warning...it's a couple of dances, some soft drinks, but that's all. I don't want to stay out late, and other than a wedding toast, I never drink alcohol."

"Yes, Ma'm!" Kirk said saluting.

"Just don't want you to get the wrong idea. After all we hardly know each other."

"My word... Lady you sure are the defensive one. You must think me the big bad wolf."

"Looks like you read minds at least as well as you dive."

Kirk threw his head back laughing. "I promise you will have a fine good time, and I'll be on my best behavior. But I'm asking one other thing of you. Please don't mention my asking you out to George. He has a serious aversion to my dating the local girls, and I'm not quite sure how he feels about the clientele."

"You mean I'm the first woman you've dated up here? Now, come on, Kirk, give me a break."

Kirk grinned. "That's correct."

"Well, if it's true, and I guess I'll have to take your word on that...I'm very flattered."

"On my honor," Kirk replied dramatically, covering his heart with his hand.

"You can relax, Kirk. I said yes."

"Good. All settled. So I'll see you tonight at about eight?"

"That should work out."

"I'll pick you up."

"What about George?"

Kirk threw his towel over his shoulder. "He and Aunt Lillian have their golf banquet tonight in Warrensburg. Our neighbor, Andy Richards, from down the road, is going to come up and watch the front desk till ten. He'll close up."

"I'll see you later then."

"Eight o'clock," Kirk repeated over his shoulder as he rounded the hedges.

Tena swam three laps, and later stood longer in the shower than usual. Afterwards, she snuggled herself into her bulky white terry cloth robe and lay on the bed, plumping up the pillows behind herself. She sorted postcards purchased during the week and wrote a few lines into her journal. The postcards made her think about the old cards exchanged between her parents and the photo of the three boys. She had brought several of these old items along with her. As she went through the mementos of her mother and father's past, each and every one tugged at her curiosity and her heart.

She didn't know why, but she also brought along the brown leather folder containing her father's military discharge papers that documented the where and the when of that horrific segment of his life. She began wondering again about what George had said the first day she arrived. Another opportunity to talk hadn't come.

Her mother said that her father never spoke of the time he spent overseas, but she knew that fight had changed him in a way that wasn't for the better. If Ben Waldron were alive today what would he have thought about this terrible Vietnam conflict that had killed American guys left and right? She could imagine what he would think of the demonstrations against the War.

As her mother often pointed out, some things didn't change. Not talking was still a constant for returning soldiers. When questioned about Saigon, Cousin Dan had uttered one word: "Hellhole."

It was pretty sick that the government wouldn't recognize Vietnam as a War. She wondered how Bobby Stein's mom felt about that idea when Bobby came home in a box a few months after her husband died. Bobby was only nineteen... Mrs. Stein's only son.

She didn't mention anything to Kirk, but she was very disappointed when at dinner the previous Saturday night, George had nothing further to contribute to his recollections of her father. His sudden distant politeness seemed to her to be very odd, and in fact, she had gotten the impression all evening that he was avoiding her. She never had the opportunity to press him further, but she hadn't given up yet.

Tena thought George's wife friendly enough when engaged in conversation, but their exchanges were always brief, and Lillian seemed nervously elusive. The behavior of both her hosts had rather surprised her after George's enthusiastic welcome the day she arrived at the inn. She couldn't put her finger on it, yet there was a weird atmosphere floating around the room that night. She knew that she hadn't done anything at all to be offensive, but something about her definitely bothered these people.

She picked up an old Valentine's Day card...opened it and stared at her father's signature. She had asked for help from above and God was listening. She was sure of that because she had come a long way in a short time with all of her investigative work, despite George.

On Monday, while Kirk had awaited poolside, she had driven to the county seat at Warrensburg. There a clerk had assisted her in accessing the Waldron family records. She had learned that her grandfather had sold the old Bowery lands to the Hendrickson Corporation, then a newly formed company specializing in land development.

She had gasped when she saw the amount that had been paid for the property consisting of the three hundred acres (known to those who loved it as "Heaven") and the storage buildings that went along with it. One hundred ten thousand dollars was without a doubt a healthy sum today, but that kind of money was a small fortune years ago before any of the recent land development had occurred.

Tess hadn't been far off when she had talked about the fate of the Waldron property. Henderson eventually had gone bust, but ended up selling that land to the Resorts Living Company who in time would develop one of the biggest ski facilities in the entire Northeast.

Although a price couldn't be put on what she was searching for, her discovery had refueled her curiosity. Where had all the proceeds from the sale gone? She noticed the date on her Grandfather's death certificate. According to the documents, Grandfather Hank passed on only five months after the sale transaction.

Wouldn't it only be natural that her father and uncle would have inherited from their father's estate since their mother had died two years earlier, and the two sons were the sole survivors? So what had happened to all of this money that could have helped make her widowed mother's life so much easier?

Tena hadn't slept that night, thinking that another piece of this puzzle was still out there someplace. With this in mind, she returned to Warrensburg on Tuesday morning. Her intuition was justified when she read Grandfather Henry's will. Ben and Bob Waldron had each inherited twenty-five thousand in cash from their father!

She had called her mother that night. Bertha had been stunned, insisting that there must have been some foul-up in the courthouse records. "I was back there twice," she told her mother. "There's no mistake."

Right about then her mother's surprise had turned angry. "You were his child, Tena. If there was an inheritance it should have come to you, and it would have been put aside for your education. Good heavens, as it stands you'll be paying off your student loans for another three years. If he had that kind of money he might have saved something for you, and then he died so unexpectedly. It could be that an account is laying dormant someplace and you could lay claim to it. Maybe we should get a lawyer to investigate all of this," Bertha remarked pensively.

"I never gave my student loans a thought, but regardless, my grandfather's will was executed almost twenty-six years ago, close to when I was born."

Bertha had sighed, saying that she supposed such an endeavor would be a useless cause after all this time. She suggested lamely that Ben could have drunk it all away...to which Tena replied, "Twenty-five thousand dollars would have bought more beer than any army could drink." In the end they had agreed to discuss it further when Tena returned home.

Mom had once told her that her father didn't own a car when they first were married. In fact they had met sharing a cab ride. Her mother had said that they were living on love in those days. Times were rough, but she insisted that they didn't pay a lot of attention to the lack of amenities in their coldwater flat where they rented on Pearl Street. She had said that the floors were slanted, and it was so cold in the house in the winter you could see your breath. That was the way they were, and now Tena was discovering that her father probably had twenty-five thousand dollars sitting in a bank. It seemed that the more she knew, the less she understood. Nothing made a bit of sense.

Several times on Tuesday night she tried to call Kay, but the line was constantly busy. She guessed that her mother must have called her first born as soon as she hung up with her, so she gave up. And now it was really too late in the week, what was the point – she'd be home on Saturday. She picked up the old Valentine's Day card that her father had sent to her mom. *Why would a man who affectionately signs a card to his wife, "Your Big Lug" and seems to have inherited a good sum of money, allow her and their small child to grovel in poverty?* She dozed off with the memorabilia scattered around her on top of the bedspread.

Chapter 10

Easing her black Camero through wide open, iron gates, Tena continued up the crushed stone incline past the stoic white pillars that so eloquently caged the nursing home's veranda. She caught a quick glimpse of Tess Waldron waiting patiently in her wheelchair on the porch. As she parked, she suddenly found herself wondering what her aunt had been like as a young woman full of expectations, and if any copies of the book she had written so long ago had survived. Tena grimaced, glancing at her Seiko. It was already quarter to five. She had napped far too long this afternoon.

Approaching the porch, she fought the queasy feeling that had been brewing, hating to think about the strong possibility that her father had failed her mother far beyond his alcoholism. Obviously, her mother had never taken her own mother's advice about life to heart. It seemed to her that she had reached into Grandma Honey's pickle barrel and made a bitter choice when falling in love with Ben Waldron.

As Tena ascended the porch steps, the elder woman leaned forward, "Oh, Tena, I'm so glad to see you." Accompanying her greeting, a cool breeze rose unexpectedly, ruffling the soft folds of her loose fitting silk dress. The delicate pattern of tiny pink carnations floated within the shimmering blue material rustling gently around the woman's thin legs. Obviously chilled, Tess pulled her white crocheted sweater together, buttoning the top round pearl buttons.

"Hi, I guess I'm late?"

"No, you're not late. I suppose I'm just an eager beaver. Why did you think that you were late, dear?"

"Because I saw you sitting up here all alone, and the way you were anxiously gesturing toward me, I thought that I must have lost track of the time."

"No dear, you're fine," Tess said, the trace of a smile emerging. "They – the keepers inside that is – don't start serving our dinners until five-thirty sharp. The warden lets me out here occasionally. Tonight I insisted. I wanted to be the first to greet my guests."

"How nice that you wanted to do that for me."

Tess continued, "The weather is so lovely this evening, don't you know. You know, I think that the head Gestapo woman has forgotten where I am." Tess winked mischievously behind thick-rimmed glasses.

Noticing Tess's mod, pink lip-gloss and her rhinestone with pink pearl earrings, obviously meant to coordinate, Tena complimented, "You look very glamorous this evening, Aunt Tess."

"Thank you, dear. I think you look very nice too. You know, I can't get over how much you resemble Benny."

Forcing a smile, Tena speculated who the other guests might be. "It still sounds strange to hear you say so."

Tess's face illuminated. "I look forward to that changing as we become more acquainted. By the way, did anybody tell you about our dinners?"

"No, but food seems to be high on the priority list up here in the Adirondacks."

"Supper here is very good, but I don't eat very much anymore," Tess said, staring past her at a red Volkswagen that had just pulled into the driveway. "There was a time when I was a good size woman. I had quite an appetite in those days, I'll tell you."

"Tess, do you want to go in now? We don't have to wait for someone to wheel you in, do we? It's getting cooler out here. I'd be happy to take you in."

"Not just yet." Tess responded quickly. Obviously trying to delay entering the house, she chattered on, returning her attention to Tena, "My mother used to make a delicious apple pie from the fruit in the orchards out back of our house. I always had a second piece. The cook here bakes a wonderful pie. Of course, nowadays I hardly get down the first slice."

"Guess nothing is as good as Mom's. Are you sure you're not cold?"

"Don't be fretting over me," Tess said, watching the driver of the Volkswagen park his car. She went on gleefully, "The air is really rather refreshing, and coupled with your company, God's good outdoors is far better for my health than those vitamin shots they give us every morning."

Tena fidgeted awkwardly for conversation, but she had joined Tess in her preoccupation with the driver who waved from the car window as he parked. "I'm sure the dinner will be awesome. Thank you for inviting me."

"Hmmm – awesome." Tess reflected as if she were opening a mental dictionary. She waved back. "That must mean the same as 'cat's meow' or 'hot stuff'?" she inquired while gazing toward the approaching visitor. Tena watched the driveway as the young man moved away from his car and began walking toward them. She mumbled absently, "Yes, that's right."

Finally, Tess announced. "My other guest has arrived."

Who the heck is this? Tena thought. "When I called you up last week to let you know I was planning to come, and you said that you had a surprise for me, you sure reeled me in. I'm a girl who can't resist a surprise."

"I'm glad to hear that, dear."

They watched as the muscular, curly haired man, dressed semi-casually in a navy blazer, approached. His step was quick, and he carried a small white box under his arm.

"Hey there, Aunt Tessie."

"Hello Johnny. I am so happy that you came. I was getting a bit worried."

"Gosh, I'm sorry. Traffic on the Northway was bumper to bumper." He bent to kiss Tess gently on the cheek. "I should have stopped off at one of the exits and given the house a call to let you know. But, you ought to know, Aunt Tess, I wouldn't miss one of your good invites."

Tess chuckled. "That's perfectly fine. You're here now."

"Hello," he said smiling at Tena.

Fascinated, Tena wondered at the familiarity of the stranger toward her Aunt while Tess made introductions. "Tena honey, this is Johnny Van Ness, your brother. Johnny this is your beautiful sister, Tena Waldron."

Tena was stunned and awkwardly mute. She thought that her legs must be as limp as her elderly Aunt's. Johnny's warm, violet blue eyes grew serious. He quickly reached for her hand. "I'm happy to know you, Tena."

"Hello, "Tena whispered, barely able to regain her voice. She clasped Johnny's calloused hand.

"I've looked forward to meeting you," Johnny said.

Confused, Tena glanced between Tess and Johnny. "I'm sorry to be coming off like a goof, but I guess…well, I guess Aunt Tess really gave me the granddad of all surprises."

"You like surprises. Remember?" Tess imposed laughingly.

Johnny grinned shyly. "Oh, boy. Your expression tells me that you didn't have the slightest notion that I would be here this evening, and you're really feeling as if you'd like to fly away right about now."

Tess formed her lips into a mock pout. "Goodness, I hope you two won't be mad at me now. I was afraid that you wouldn't want to come, Tena, if I told you that I had invited Johnny, and I didn't know how you would feel, Johnny, about me not saying anything to Tena."

"I'm not at all angry, Aunt Tess, and…" Tena faced Johnny, "I'm not one to run from anything."

"Well, that's good news." He returned his attention to Tess. "I brought you a little something," he said, offering her the small, white, ribbon-tied box.

"Why thank you. Oh my word! You are such the gentleman. I haven't had one of these in years," she exclaimed withdrawing an orchid corsage. "But, you shouldn't have been so extravagant."

Johnny laughed, apparently delighted that he had pleased Tess so much.

"Oh, isn't that gorgeous," Tena whispered. "Now we must go inside. Aunt Tess, you might be filled with that formidable Adirondack pioneer spirit, but this flower knows only warmth, so we had better go in or the poor thing will freeze," Tena emphasized.

Tena's suggestion came none too soon. A heavy-set, middle-aged woman dressed in a crisp, white uniform, stepped from the double oak doorway onto the veranda. "Lord, my goodness, look what you have there, Tess. I see you're not only lucky at the Bingos."

Feigning shock, Tess spouted, "Don't let her kid you, I am no fan of the Bingo," she said replacing the orchid into the box. "These are my guests for dinner, Lilah: I'd like you to meet Tena Waldron and Johnny Van Ness."

"How do you do, folks? Now, Tess, you've been sittin' out there for almost an hour. You were of a mind that I wouldn't have noticed, but I've had my eye on you."

"Oh, I knew you would get around to me pretty soon now," Tess replied flippantly.

"You and me are going to bring these young folks into the house before they catch the shivers. There is nothin' worse than a summer cold. You know people come up to visit, and they just don't know that it gets darn cold up here in these mountains. Dinner is going to be served in fifteen minutes. Everybody else is already sittin' at their tables, and they are all wonderin' what's happened to you."

Tess sighed, "When someone doesn't show up for dinner," she said to Tena, "everyone holds their breath, if you get my drift."

"I get your drift."

"Okay, ladies" Johnny ordered amicably, "Let's show them all we're alive and kickin'. Come on, Tessie, loosen your brakes, and hold on for the ride!" Tess giggled girlishly, grabbing the side arms of the wheelchair.

Minutes later, Tess and her young company were seated beside two other residents of the home; Olive Picken, a retired elementary school teacher and widow of an upstate local judge, and Miss Florence Long, also a retired school teacher who was originally from Albany. After Tena was introduced they began gingerly passing dishes heaped with food.

"Thank you, Tena, for helping me pin on my corsage."

"You're welcome. I brought you something myself," Tena replied, reaching into her clutch bag. Here – it's one that my mother embroidered. She said to say hello, and hopes that you're in good health. She said to tell you that she'd try to make a visit up before the summer is over."

"Oh, how lovely!" Tess exclaimed as she examined Bertha's gift of a rose-stitched handkerchief. "Please thank her for me."

"Goodness, it looks like they pulled out all the stops tonight, Olive. We've got the royal English lace cloth on the table," Florence remarked.

"Cap Morgan from the bank is over there," Olive replied, pointing to a table on the far side of the room. "The Administrator must be in need of another donation."

Florence glanced over her shoulder and raised her brow apprehensively; "He makes me nervous when he shows up. I'm always afraid they will change things, maybe even shut down the place the way they did Butterfield."

Tena tried not to be conspicuous as she scrutinized the freckled, sandy haired, young man seated across from her who was accepted by her aunt to be her estranged brother. Her mother had her reservations, but Johnny's hair was only a shade off from her own, and she had noticed almost immediately that he had those Waldron dimples.

He could be my brother, she thought. As she considered the complexity of the possibility, the knot in her stomach grew.

"I've lived in these wonderful Adirondack Mountains a good number of years, but I've never seen the black flies as bad as they are this year," Florence complained.

Tess moved around in her chair uncomfortably. "Now Flo, lets not talk about those pests. You don't see any in the dining room, do you?"

"I'm just commenting; that's all. Turning to Tena she said, "They have a lovely garden here, but you can't be out there more than five minutes to enjoy it."

"Well, I hope that they calm down soon, but it's funny that they are up here. I've used the pool a couple of times at the inn and don't believe I've been bothered by one."

"How very odd," Florence replied dubiously. "Mr. Van Ness, would you kindly pour me a glass of lemonade from that pitcher?"

"Yes, of course, but, remember, you can call me Johnny."

"Oh, yes, indeed, I remember now. Did Tess tell you that I taught school for over fifty years, though I'm not as old, mind you, as your Aunt?"

"Yes, I believe you told me that you had been a teacher the last time I visited."

Tena glanced dubiously at Florence.

Tess rustled in her chair. "You make me sound as if I were around with the country's founding fathers while you were just a slip of a girl when Roosevelt was in office. Florence, you know perfectly well that you're older than I."

"I stand corrected, Tess dear," Florence replied. Smiling at Johnny, she added, "I think I'd like another small spoonful of peas, if you don't mind."

Johnny reached for the bowl. "My pleasure."

"She loves to be waited on," Olive commented without taking her eyes from her plate as Johnny gingerly added a spoonful of vegetable.

"I do not!"

"Let us not argue with one another in front of guests," Tess pleaded softly.

"I apologize, Flo. I'm afraid that I'm a bit out of sorts this evening. I'm sorry."

"Never mind, Olive, I shouldn't be so sensitive. We're usually quite the gay bunch," Florence said addressing Tena. "And truly, we are very happy that you both accepted Tess's invitation. All she has talked about is getting you two acquainted."

"Yes, Olive chimed in. "It's such a pleasure to have a man at the table, especially one as handsome as you are, Johnny. Did anyone ever tell you that you look just like Robert Redford?"

"Oh, for heavens sake, Olive," Tess flustered.

Johnny tried not to laugh, but there was no mistaking the flush that came over him. "You ladies do like to flatter a guy."

Tena had a thousand questions that were tripping over one another inside of her head, but she was finding it extremely difficult to put any into a rational query. To begin with, her supposed brother seemed nice, but what was he really after? It was clear that he had been here several times, yet Tess had indicated when they met previously that she hardly ever saw him. Tess was quite advanced in years, so it could be that she didn't remember well, or maybe there was something that she didn't want known.

As if he were reading her mind, Johnny said, "I came up to see Aunt Tess a few times after my Uncle Buck died. We had bumped into one another at his wake."

"That's right," Tess interjected.

Johnny said, "I guess it's true what folks say about only getting together with the relatives at weddings and funerals. Anyway, I hadn't seen her since I was a boy, and she was gracious enough to give a single guy a chance at some good cooking."

Tena accepted the bowl of peas. "Now I see."

"See what, Dear?" Olive asked.

"I have to say that all of what has happened to me during the last few weeks has been so unexpected. Being here right now would never have happened if I hadn't stopped by Smith's in North Creek for a sandwich…"

Olive cautiously interrupted Tena, but directed her question to Tess. "Isn't Smith's a bar?"

Tess replied, "They serve food as well as cocktails. Smith's was always a grand place to dine."

"That is true," Flo added. "I've been there myself with my niece, Noreen. In fact, she took me there for dinner last month. Remember, Olive, I told you all about it? The truth be known, where can anyone go in our area for a nice dinner?"

Wistfully Olive said, "The judge, God bless him, always took me to Russell Roost or Hideaway Hills."

Tess dropped one lump of sugar into the cup of tea that an attendant had just set down in front of her. "Russell Roost, I'm afraid, is long gone, and Hideaway Hills is far too pricy for young people just starting out to frequent. So, go on, Dear."

Tena patted Olive's arm reassuringly. "Don't worry, Olive, I seldom drink alcohol, and I entered through the restaurant entrance. But, I'll tell you that it's a long trip up from home to North Creek, and I was very hungry that day."

"I hope that you have been enjoying your vacation away from work. Are you enjoying the inn?"

"Yes, very much."

"Good. That's very good," Tess said thoughtfully.

"It seems though that I have gathered more questions than I have answers."

"Oh?" Tess replied.

"I hope you don't mind, but I've brought along that old photograph I showed you the last time I was up." Tena handed the snapshot to Johnny. Turning toward Tess, Tena said, "You picked out my father and my uncle in the photo and thought the other boy was Buck Van Ness. Remember, Aunt Tess? Would that be your relation, Johnny?"

"I don't know," Johnny said looking at the picture. "It could be Uncle Buck, but Uncle Buck was balding, the way I remember him. I'm not much help with old family stuff. I wasn't raised around here, and unfortunately neither my mother nor my step-dad ever wanted to bother much with any of their relatives. We didn't see much of Uncle Buck."

Tess whispered to Florence, "that would be Elsie's son-in-law, I'd imagine."

"I bet I'd know who's in your picture," Olive said smugly. "I've got a good memory for faces, especially those who were my students. I recall your father too, Tena".

"You do?"

"Oh, yes. He liked to take his fishing pole down to the creek when he was supposed to be in my class. He was a bit of a wanderer, but he wasn't a bold boy."

Tena smiled. "Thank goodness."

Florence said, "School lessons in those days were taught in one large room with those who were little more than babies sitting beside the elder children right until they went to the high school. That's how it was with all of them sharing the same space, learning from different books. But the children were well taught all the same."

Olive piped up, "Yes, we didn't get the new schools in this area until the fifties. Of course, the old high school burned down, and then they built that new one. Tess, do you remember when Gunther's Livery Boarding and Delaba Stables were next door to the old one room school house?"

"Indeed I do," Tess chuckled. "Goodness, talk about flies, what flies we suffered with during the springtime in those days. But, I suppose the liverymen didn't notice. So you ought not complain, Olive, as you know the flies are never as bad as back then."

Olive studied Tess over her glasses. "But you and I both know, Tess, that all Adirondack flies are not the same. Like everything else up here, the flies are all cousins to one another."

"I don't know what you mean," Tess replied.

"Let me have a look at your photo, Tena," Olive insisted. Tena passed her the black and white photograph. "Yes, that's them. Who wouldn't recognize that troop? They were always together."

Tess whispered to Tena, "Yes, of course it's them, just as I told you. That's Buck Van Ness, I'm quite sure."

"You know," Olive said, "if you would like to visit the old school sometime I could arrange it. My niece, Kelly, turned the building into a nursery school, which was an idea readily embraced by everyone in town, or so I've been told. It had been vacant for quite awhile and needed some fixing to be sure, but some of the locals who are handy with a hammer came forward to help her, and it was done. Once a month I volunteer as a reader for story hour. I would be happy to give Kelly a call and introduce you two."

"Thank you, I would enjoy seeing where my father went to school. Of course, meeting the little people and your niece would be nice as well. Just let me know far enough ahead so that I can take an afternoon off from work and come up."

"Really the fifties?" Johnny mused.

"Yes, as I said, the children didn't get separated until they went on to the high school," Olive said.

"Many things changed here after the war," Tess reflected. "The young men who came home did so praising the Lord for their survival...rightly so. Naturally, they wanted to pick up the pieces, take hold of their wives and those children that up till then they had never seen. They needed to get on with their lives.

"Our government was extremely eager for them to put this country back together, and so that was how all those little houses in Warren County came about, and also how the big new school was built."

"You know, it fascinates me to think about all those kids in one room learning lessons at different levels," Tena said.

"Of course," Olive said, "when I think of the new school I'm put in mind of the old one where Kelly is now. There is a gas station on the spot where the livery used to be next to the old school. The horses are missed, but not those flies!"

Tena couldn't contain herself a second longer. She turned to Johnny, "So what draws you to North Creek? You said you came for your Uncle's funeral. I mean, as for myself, I was more curious than anything else. I hardly knew my father, which is the real reason I'm here tonight I guess. He died when I was six."

Johnny said addressing Tena, "I didn't know my birth father, your dad, at all," but I was pretty much raised by a super step-dad, so I can't say as a kid I felt as though I was missing anything, but...well, I guess I'm the same as you, Tena, wanting to touch base."

Tess sipped her tea. "You can't imagine how delighted I am that all this worked out so well. Isn't it funny how God brings His people together? I must admit that I often wonder why the Good Lord has left me here so long, and then, just when I assume that He's done with me, He gives me another chore. Here I hadn't seen Johnny since he was a small boy, and then Buck passed on. Of course, Buck Van Ness was a grand man who is still missed, but you know the expression, when one door closes another opens. That was exactly what happened, and so I feel something good has come out of his death because next thing I knew you came visiting. When Tena came to see me it just seemed only right that I have you two meet."

Florence and Olive chuckled. "Oh my, Tess, you are a card," Olive said. "She's always arranging something, and very clever too how she does it."

"Now, Olive, don't get carried away." Tess admonished.

Tena interjected, "Today we call someone who arranges people and events or meetings, a 'networker'. I think Johnny would agree there's nothing wrong with networking when the process reunites a family."

"Absolutely!" Johnny agreed.

"Oh, come on," Tess said to Olive and Florence, "we may as well say hello to the banker. Will you two excuse us? Olive rose from the table and Florence followed, wheeling Tess's chair across the room.

After a moment Johnny leaned over the table. "It's a lot to digest."

"I beg your pardon?"

"This family thing, the old roots who-ha," Johnny said, encouraging both dimples. "Let's be real – it's a little weird."

"Yes, it's every bit of that, but you know, even though I'm confused, I'm not sorry I came. Are you?"

Johnny paused thoughtfully. "No, actually I'm not. I'm here out of pure curiosity, nothing sinister. I say this because I've gotten the feeling all through dinner that you think I'm poaching on your territory or something. To be honest, I don't feel one way or another about Ben Waldron. Paul Van Ness legally adopted me. Ben Waldron was never in my life. Paul was my dad."

Tena flushed, "I think you're reading..."

"I don't think I'm misreading anything here. Just let me finish. My adopted folks died in a car crash years ago, and the only family that showed up at their services was Uncle Buck. I owed it to him to come up for his service when he died, and that was the first I'd been up here in years."

"Why weren't you curious before then? I mean, didn't you ever visit North Creek without a reason?"

"Did you?"

"No."

"So there you have it," Johnny said.

"Well, I guess we both had reasons," Tena said relaxing against the back of her chair. "In my case my mother never drove, and I never got a license until I was almost twenty. I took the bus whenever I needed to be somewhere, and digging up old family roots wasn't first priority in those days. In fact, until recently, it wasn't at the top of my list at all. But, you have to admit it's kind of strange that we both end up here at the same time."

"Coincidence," Johnny said. "I've come to see Tess several times since we met at my Uncle's wake. I imagine that you got the gist of that soon after we sat down to dinner. I felt sorry for the old girl at first, and thought I'd do a good deed and come see her at the home, but now I look forward to visiting. She's a neat person. I'll tell you she really amazes me with all the old stories she has in her head. I don't think that I have a memory like she does. It's just something to know her."

"I apologize for grilling you, Johnny. It's clear to me now that my diabolical, nutty mind ran away with me."

Johnny grinned. "I just wanted to set things straight. I'd like us to be friends."

"I would too. And to set things straight on my end, I never knew Ben Waldron either. I do have some vague memories, but he passed away when I was so small, and to be truthful my mother had left him a couple of years before he died. I just think it's all very sad when people miss the boat in relationships. Nobody ever knows what could have been."

Johnny responded, "So, the two of us are chasing phantoms instead of rainbows."

"I guess you could put it that way."

Johnny stood as the ladies returned to the table, and then assisted each nestling in. "We've done our civic duty," Olive said quietly. "How did you two fare without us?"

"Just great," Johnny replied.

Tena observed Johnny carefully. Her mother was right. Everybody doesn't need to know everything. It was time to loosen up and allow her instincts to kick in. Brother or no...

he appeared to be a decent man. She turned toward Tess, "I'm so glad I came this evening."

"Have you been to the Waldron family plot?" Johnny asked.

"Yes, I finally found it the Sunday morning after I arrived, and I placed a wreath on my father's marker, but while I was up there I noticed that half the cemetery is filled with Waldron headstones."

"Yeah, there's a lot of them. I was thinking that maybe we could get together sometime and pay our joint respects...if you feel that would be appropriate?"

"I think that would be nice."

"Wouldn't Ben and Buck be pleased," Tess said. The other women nodded in agreement.

"You know," Tena said, "maybe one of you could help me with a little mystery I encountered on my way up to North Creek last Saturday."

Olive brightened, "I adore a good mystery."

The three leaned closer to hear Tena's details. "I really was turned around when I drove up here. My first intent was to visit my father's grave, but I ended up stopping off at a different cemetery...a very old graveyard near Bossardsville."

"Oh, dear," said Olive. "You really were off track."

Florence said, "It's a shame about that old cemetery out there. Nobody ever takes care of it."

"I agree, Flo, but who is left to do it?" Olive said contemplatively. "It has been years since anyone was buried out there, and so it is understandable that no one is left to care for the final resting place of those poor souls. But, that's how it goes. People move away. They forget."

Tena quickly spoke up, "That's not all together true. There are still people who care about loved ones buried up there.

I met one while I was hiking around looking for Waldron names. The lady said that her husband was buried there. She also pointed me in the direction of the only Waldron grave in the cemetery, which, believe me, I would never have found on my own."

Tess stared at Tena. "Who would that be?" she asked."

"I read the tombstone. Garret Waldron died on July 3rd, nearly two hundred years ago. I recall the date because I was fascinated that I was there reading his epitaph on July 3rd. Interesting, don't you think?"

All conversation came to an immediate halt, the silence broken after a long pause by Olive. "You must have misunderstood who this woman was visiting. You say it was her husband?"

"Yes."

"You're sure she said that her husband was buried there," Tess asked less critically.

Tena didn't understand what could have come over the three of them. "Yes, she said she had come for her husband. I am one hundred percent sure that was what she said."

"Oh...glory be," Tess mused. "But, you mentioned before that you needed help with a mystery?"

"Yes, well, maybe I was just a little over dramatic. Seems to be my nature," Tena said, glancing at Johnny. "It was just so strange how she disappeared that's all. One minute she was there with me, but when I looked up she was gone...no car or anything in sight. I'm curious if there is a housing development close that she could have walked to, but maybe hidden behind the trees?"

Olive fidgeted. "Now settle down," Tess reprimanded. "Tena, Did the woman give her name? Was she an older woman?"

Tena sighed. "I'm embarrassed to say that I never did get her name, but I'd say that she was about fifty. She did say that she belonged to the Church that had been there awhile ago."

Florence was ashen colored. She put down her fork, shoving her piece of pie aside. "This is not possible," she said. "That church this woman spoke of was Trinity Church, and it burned now near to sixty years ago. I remember the fire well. My grandmother and grandfather were married in that little church, and I can still see my grandmother crying as we stood by the charred ruins.

"It was a small congregation and it took the church members quite some time to raise the money for a new church. When enough building funds were secured, it was decided to construct the new church on Phillips Street over on the opposite side of the town. I know all about all of this because I'm a member of the new Trinity church. Tess is also a member. Ethel Fortin is good enough to take us to services once a month. In recent years membership has dwindled down to next to nothing, so it's no wonder the old graveyard is neglected."

"I'm Catholic," Olive interjected quietly. "Father McKinney is my cousin."

"Wait a minute," Johnny said. "Now, I'm the confused one. "Tena you talked with a woman whose husband is buried there, but no one has been interred for over sixty years? You must have heard her wrong."

"I think that's what she said. Yes, in fact, I'm sure that she said that she was going to be by her husband. Maybe I just mistook her meaning. Maybe she went someplace else to meet him or something. The truth is I was so preoccupied I didn't actually see where she went."

Tess said casually, "When anyone passes they are either buried in the Union Cemetery, where your father is, in the Methodist one, or at the Catholic Cemetery, and all three places are right here in North Creek."

Regaining her composure, "Olive said, "I'm sure it was one of those women with the historical society who come up every so often from Albany. They have a peculiar interest in taking a charcoal rubbing of the stones. They have been doing that sort of thing for years. I think the practice disgraceful. Most likely, that was the case, and this mystery woman went to meet her husband at someplace nearby."

"Perhaps," Tess remarked thoughtfully, "it was Ruth Wilson. I think her husband is buried there."

"Ruth is over ninety if she's a day, and she can hardly walk, "Florence barked.

Lilah came by offering more pie, which all except Johnny declined. He had been listening intently to the batter between the women, waiting for the perfect opening which had finally presented itself. "It sounds to me ladies as if this mystery is solved. Tena has seen a ghost."

"Ooh, my word, such a thing to say. Don't you know there are no ghosts?" Tess admonished.

"Listen everybody," Lilah interjected "I think who this young lady saw was no ghost, but that woman we've been readin' about in the papers lately."

"Who do you mean?" Olive asked.

"I don't know, some woman who lives on the outskirts of town with her father and goes botherin' people – knockin' on their doors at all hours, tellin' them strange stuff."

"Sounds like a ghost to me," Johnny persisted kiddingly. "What do you think, Olive?"

"I think that you're both trying to pull some old gals' legs. That's what you two had your heads together about while we were over there dispensing our pleasantries."

Johnny laughed. "Hey Tena, when you finally located the Union Cemetery did you get a chance to look around at the *really* old graves there?"

"What old graves? Oh, yes, I did a few days later," Tena replied, though her thoughts were so scattered that she hardly absorbed his question. "To tell you the truth, I think my experience that first day up here scared me, so I'll wait until we go together."

"Since you like this kind of thing, I have a feeling that you would find a thorough walk through the Union Cemetery interesting. I hadn't been there either until Uncle Buck died. I lingered there for a little while after the service and walked around. I discovered generations of families buried together. Kind of gives you a nice feeling of continuity in this crazy world."

Olive smiled. "It's a blessed gesture."

Johnny leaned toward Tena, "How about this Saturday?"

"Saturday might be okay if I get back early enough. I'm not planning to go home until very early Sunday morning. I don't know if I mentioned it, but I'm staying over at the Pine Cone Inn."

"Oh goodness, what a lovely place," Florence chirped in with wild abandon – obviously happy to have parted with her thoughts of gruesome graves and ghosts, "I imagine that you feel like a contestant on "Queen for a Day" with Lillian fussing over you. Of course, I've never stayed overnight there, but I had dinner there with my ladies club a few years back. I was honored as a lifetime member."

Tess leaned toward Florence. "I already told you that she was staying at the Pine Cone."

"It's very nice," Tena agreed.

"Are you also staying at the Pine Cone, Johnny?" Tess queried.

"No, I'm driving back to Kingston tonight."

"That's nearly a two hour drive," Tena commented.

"I don't mind," he said, addressing Tena. "I enjoy driving at night. It gives me quiet time to sort out my thoughts. I haven't had such an interesting evening in ages. No doubt about it, tonight was well worth the commute."

"You're nice to say so," Tena said.

"Not nice, just honest.   Anyway, I have to get back. My partner and I are working a good size project near Poughkeepsie. It's a penalty job, and the owner is pressing for completion. That means that every day that we miss the projected completion date to finish, we will be charged two hundred dollars. But, I'm sure that I can see my way clear to get back into town this Saturday. I could take a room over at the Holiday Inn in Lake George. That way I'd have more time to do the ancestral thing, and if you're up for it, I'll buy all you gals a great dinner. That is, if you'd care to join me."

Tess said, "That is very gentlemanly of you to offer, but you children go ahead. We'll take you up on your invitation another time."

"That's right," Olive agreed. "Sometime in the future on a Sunday afternoon would be delightful. Wouldn't you think so, Flo?"

Florence nodded. "I will say though that this has been a grand time together."

Tess chimed in, "I agree, and I hope that you have forgiven me, Tena?"

"Yes, of course, and don't give it another thought. I was pleasantly surprised, and it certainly has been an awakening."

Johnny and Tena got up from the table and made their way around to each of the women still seated there, saying their good-byes to each in turn.

As they turned toward the doorway, Tess grabbed Tena's hand, "You will stop by and see us again before leaving town, won't you?"

Tena promised that she would.

On the porch Johnny said, "Look, Tena, I really am glad that we've met. Here's my business card. I wear a beeper, and Sally, that's our girl in the office, she can get through to me if you change your mind about Saturday."

Tena took the card, "Thanks, I don't see a problem, but if anything comes up and I can't make it, I'll call your office."

"Sounds like a plan."

Chapter 11

A sign on the wall of the upper deck of the Minne-Ha-Ha, one of the Adirondack's oldest and most respected tourist boats, silently testified that Lake George is two hundred thirty feet deep, nearly thirty-two miles long, and that parts of the lake measure three miles wide.

Standing beside Kirk, Tena bent over the Minne's side rail watching the impressive paddle wheel do its work, thinking how the lake might have been when first discovered by the French explorers. *It had to be really something back in those times. No wonder that Samuel de Champlain wrote about it in his journal.* She glanced up into the heavens.

"Well, Kirk, here we are, and it's *Christmas in July*," she whispered.

"Excuse me?"

"Nothing. I was just thinking about how full the sky is tonight with stars, and how the history of Lake George has always captivated me."

"How so?"

"You probably don't know that the lake was named as a tribute to a King. That would have been the English King, George II. Just a bit of old, New York trivia that's popped into my head. Maybe you can use it in your next brochure."

Kirk smiled. "That's a possibility, and no, I didn't know, but I must admit I was astonished to read how massive the lake is in size."

"I noted that too, pretty impressive."

"My Aunt Lillian and I did visit Fort William Henry awhile back. She had been there with George many years ago. I've always had an interest in American History, especially the Colonial Period, and I found the excursion quite interesting. Of course, we're not much on Northern history in Virginia."

"I won't hold it against you. Other than watching *Gone With The Wind* a half dozen times, I don't know much about Southern history."

"What a night," Kirk expelled, slipping his arm around her.

Tena looked up again at the sky. There were millions of stars surrounding that full-faced, midsummer moon. The glitz of the celestial dome high above really did twinkle like holiday ornaments. "Did you ever wonder where we go when we leave this planet?"

"I assume that you're referring to life after death?"

"Yes"

After a moment of thought, Kirk answered, "I was raised a Christian, but I'm afraid that I'm a rather lame one. I don't believe in much of an afterlife. And you?"

"Oh, I have no doubt that there's far more for us than what we can see, and I sure hope that heaven is like I picture it."

Without speaking, Kirk lifted one of her hands to his lips, kissing her fingers gently, and every nerve that God had given to her awoke. *This is ridiculous*, she thought. *I hardly know him.* But, she could hear the galloping beat of her heart. Red faced, she hoped that her feelings wouldn't be exposed by the moonlight and, pulling her hand away, resumed her grip on the smooth varnished oak railings, shifting her focus to the black waters below.

As the boat swayed, Kirk stepped behind her, bracing her body with his own. Encircling her with his arms, he leaned his chin on the crown of her head. This time she made no attempt to dissuade him, allowing him to join her in viewing the lights of the homesites that lined the opposite side of the lake. They were silent, as were the other passengers on the open deck, listening to the distant sounds of land bound tourists. Noticing her knuckles were white from holding the rail so tensely, he whispered, "Trust me."

"Kirk..."

"What's the matter?"

"Remember what I told you. Really, I don't want....."

"I know, and I feel the same way. Let's just enjoy ourselves."

Tena continued to stare ahead. "No, you don't know. I almost didn't meet you tonight, but I'm glad that I did."

"You were going to stand me up? You would have broken my heart."

"I seriously doubt that your heart is that easily broken, but yes, I considered standing you up. I've just got an awful lot on my mind. It has nothing to do with you. Anyway, I'm here, so I guess it was meant to be."

Kirk turned her around, facing her squarely. "So, I'm forgiven for not being able to get us in tonight?"

"To be candid, I'm glad that we couldn't get into Bo Jam Bo's. As it turns out, I'm really not in the mood for the blare of that kind of place this evening. What band could possibly beat all of this?"

Kirk pulled her to him. "I'm happy you're not disappointed. I'd like to add that I'm not disappointed either. You've made this night magical. I don't think that you have the vaguest idea of how much I'm attracted to you."

"I'm beginning to guess," Tena replied nervously.

"I'd like to reach right up there and pull down one of those stars for you, but even if I could, not one of them would outshine you. Not one!" Kirk attested enthusiastically pointing upwards.

"You're very nice, and I'm very flattered."

"I don't mean to embarrass you, Tena, but I can't imagine that a girl as gorgeous as you are hasn't heard this before. I mean it. You're a living Fourth of July sparkler."

"Oh, come on."

"It's no line."

"Well, thank you, but I'm just a regular, ordinary girl."

"Here's my answer to ordinary." His kiss was hard and deep.

"Kirk!" She pushed him away. "Please, don't spoil what up until now has been a super evening."

Kirk put his hands on both her shoulders. "Okay, you can say it. 'Kirk, you're out of bounds.' And you might be right, but how can any guy help it with a beauty like you this close."

"Kirk."

"All right, I'll simmer down. Again, my apology. But, I promise you, Miss Waldron, that the day will come when I'll be taking you to Bo Jam Bo's for raw clams and some of their famous fried chicken. And I won't let you slip away, that's a promise. That is, if you still care to go with me after my heart made me lose my head."

"Maybe, but it would be just clams and chicken. Do you comprehend?"

"I've overstepped, I understand," Kirk whispered into her ear, apologetically.

Tena flushed. "Yes, you have. I don't mean to say that…"

"I understand," he repeated putting his finger to her lips.

She felt herself losing ground. It was difficult to resist Kirk Morehouse's allure, but at the pool her heart had told her head not to accept this date. *I have to stop listening to my heart and start using my head,* she thought.

"You have to understand, I'm only human," Kirk pleaded while surveying her pensively. Her long red hair floated out like a burning flame behind her in the balmy summer breeze, and, without thinking, he gave in to an overwhelming urge to redirect a few small strands that had blown over to the side of her mouth.

"I'm sorry. Please don't get the idea that I don't like you. It's just…"

Kirk folded his hands solemnly on the railing. "You know, you haven't said a word about your dinner earlier. You were going to visit an elderly aunt, I believe."

"Yes, Aunt Tess."

"If you'd like to talk, I'm all ears. Would you like to tell me what happened to you while dining this evening at Garnet Manor that was so devastating that we were almost cheated out of this magnificent night?"

Observing him objectively, her head wanted to have an intelligent discussion, while her heart wanted to lay her head against his chest and unburden her soul. What harm would there be in telling him a part of the story. Cautiously she began, "I met my brother today for the very first time."

"You're kidding."

"No, until about a week ago I had no idea that I had a half-brother!"

Kirk straightened up. "That's amazing, and you had no idea?"

"None," Tena offered the half-truth with a sigh. "So you can well imagine how I'm feeling right about now."

"Of, course, you probably feel like a stranger in a foreign land."

"Somewhat."

Kirk was unprepared for such a personal disclosure. Suddenly, his plan for the remainder of the evening had gone haywire, but he continued to stand politely attentive, still hoping that the evening wouldn't prove a total loss.

"Shock is an accurate observation," Tena said. "My Aunt Tess decided to surprise me with this revelation just prior to our dinner. That's another reason I'm glad we skipped our late night supper. I've still got indigestion."

Kirk had begun to resign himself to the fact that he wasn't going to get to first base on this particular night. After a few moments he asked, "What did you think of your newly discovered brother?"

"I thought that he was nice. He struck me as a good, clean-cut person, and I have no doubt whatsoever that he was just as shocked, and uncomfortable, as I was by our mutual aunt's big surprise."

Kirk threw his head back and laughed vivaciously. "I, too, would be a little uncomfortable under such circumstances."

Tena felt the back of her neck tense. "Well, this is my package to unravel. It will take time to adjust, but I'll work it out. You know what; let's just switch the conversation to your family for a little while if you don't mind."

"What about them?"

"I'm confused about something to do with your Aunt Lillian."

"What about Aunt Lil?" he asked, careful to keep a smooth tone.

"Do you know why your aunt doesn't like me?"

Kirk stepped back, obviously stunned. "Why Tena, I can assure you that Lillian MacArthur likes everyone. Why do you feel that she is making an exception with you?"

"It's not just Lillian, Kirk. Your uncle is always polite enough, but I feel like he's avoiding me. When I heard that George was in the war with my father, I got really excited because I thought that I would be able to talk with him about my dad, but whenever I try approaching him, he avoids me."

"My uncle was wounded during World War II," Kirk responded quietly. "I would think that he holds old memories inside that are just too painful for him to recall. I wouldn't worry about it. As for Lillian, I would think that she would be honored to have you at the Pine Cone considering you're a Waldron."

"What do you mean? What's so great about being a Waldron?"

Kirk eyed her curiously. "You really don't know, do you?"

"I haven't the vaguest idea."

Suddenly tired of wasting time and opportunity, Kirk said, "Let me buy you a soft-drink at the concession stand, and I'll give you an education about your ancestors," He proceeded to guide her toward the cabin door. "I suppose that I owe you an apology, Tena. I truly thought that you were playing a little game with me. When you registered, I thought that you had other reasons for choosing to stay with us at the Pine Cone, other than the regular tourist's interest in charming accommodations and a dining room offering exceptional food."

Tena whispered over her shoulder, "I don't play games, Kirk. Whatever are you talking about?"

The two descended the stairs into an informal dining area below the deck. "What would you like?" Kirk asked.

"I think just a plain Coke with ice would hit the spot."

"All right," Kirk said. "If you don't mind, would you find us a table while I go to the snack bar and place our order? It looks to me that there is a self-serve situation in here tonight. I don't believe there is a waitress."

Tena nodded and scanned the cramped room for vacant seats. Spotting two, she wove her way precariously toward them and sat down.

Kirk soon returned, "One Coke with ice for the fair lady."

"Thanks, Kirk."

"You're most welcome," Kirk replied, sipping his own black coffee. "I'd really like a good 'Manhattan'," he commented while putting the cup down in front of himself. He leaned back in his chair. "But those days are gone, and I'm working on turning over a few new leaves of my own."

"So," Tena said, not wanting to lose the opportunity to hear about her ancestors, "back to where you left off."

Kirk's dark eyes grew serious. "Do you know anything about the history of the Pine Cone Inn?"

Tena shook her head. "No, I know nothing about the inn except what was in the brochure that I read. To be honest, I've never stayed in a small, cozy inn before, and I guess I thought it would be a step away from the main stream. My father was born and raised in North Creek, and I just wanted to come up and check it all out. That was all there was to it. The place just sounded so inviting, and your rates are compatible to my pocketbook, so here I am."

"And that was all there was to you booking a room with us?"

"Yes, believe me, I'm being totally honest. All I wanted to do was get away on my own and get to know more about my father. You see, he died when I was a little girl, and I never really had the chance to know him."

"And you never heard any of the folklore about our old inn?" Kirk persisted.

Tena shook her head no again.

"Garret Waldron, a possible ancestor of yours," Kirk began, "purchased a large tract of land up near what is today the village of North Creek sometime in the mid-seventeen hundreds, I believe, near a place then called Elm Hill. We figure that one of his sons built the inn some years later. From what the old records show, the Waldron family resided originally in Schaghticoke, New York."

"Why would they have come way up here to what must have been wilderness back in those days?"

"It was the wilderness, but full of opportunity. You would be surprised," Kirk said. "From the research my aunt did on the area, it appears that Elm Hill was quite a boom town back in those days. There were several mills, and a cloth factory, and lumbering was big business. All those people working in the mills needed a place to stay."

Tena gasped, suddenly remembering her graveyard encounter on her trip up to North Creek.

"What's the matter?" Kirk asked.

"You won't believe this, but I was kneeling at the grave of a Garret Waldron the first day that I came up here. I stumbled upon it."

"Well, my word, that truly is astonishing." Kirk declared.

"Strange." Tena whispered.

"What is most strange is that as far as anyone can determine, Garret Waldron didn't live in these parts. He purchased the land, but never lived here. Some of his offspring came up, but as far as is known, Garret invested in the enterprise but never had much to do with it other than on paper. Seems to me if Aunt Lillian was aware of the founding father's gravesite, she would have told me. I've been quite taken with the history of the inn, as you can see."

"Maybe it's a different Garret Waldron buried out there on the edge of town?" Tena mused.

Kirk continued, "Waldrons were indeed here, and many are buried at the Union Cemetery, but I have no idea which of them. One of Garret's sons, William, came up with his family early in the 1800's, and we suspect that he built the inn and ran it for a while. Perhaps the old man came to live with his son's family and was buried on a farm that existed over there back then. The farms up here at one time were enormous. Large portions of land became farms to raise rye for the distillery, as well as vegetables and livestock to feed the mill workers throughout the area. There were several Waldron farms during that period."

Tena could hear her heartbeat. "Kirk, it's so weird that you bring up Garret Waldron. And my accidental visit to the graveyard and then to simply happen upon that gravesite is weirder still. But, there is more to that visit. While there I met a woman who just seemed to appear out of thin air, and it was she who brought me straight to his grave. There are far too many people that were buried near Garret for it to have been some sort of small farm plot. Besides which, this woman said that there had been a church, and one of the ladies at the nursing home confirmed that was true. I don't know," Tena sighed. "None of this makes any sense. Look at me. I have goose bumps thinking about that whole episode."

Kirk had become completely engrossed. "Perhaps there is another explanation. There is a group home in town where some of the older ladies who were residents of a downstate psychiatric facility were transferred," he said. "I understand that there was quite an uproar from the locals in the beginning, but these women are harmless enough, and are always well supervised when they come into town for their outings. I think most everyone has grown accustomed to their strangeness. Maybe one of them had wandered off."

Tena replied, "The ladies up at the nursing home suggested something along those lines, but a misplaced resident doesn't make any sense to me either. The woman I saw and talked to was not an old lady, although I'll admit she seemed a bit odd."

"That's probably it," Kirk reassured.

"No, I still don't buy that explanation. You know, I keep telling myself that everything that's happened to me since I've arrived in North Creek is just a wild coincidence, but I've got to say, I'm finding it more and more difficult to think rationally and remain calm."

Kirk sipped his coffee patiently.

"I'm sorry I interrupted you, Kirk. Please go on with the story about Garret," Tena whispered.

"When I bought into the inn, I did a great amount of research regarding the property," Kirk continued. "An inn with a history is far more enchanting than just an old place to lay one's head."

Tena laughed. "I suppose."

"Once I discovered that Garret Waldron was the grandson of one of the first pioneers of this part of New York, I knew I had something appealing."

"I recall my Aunt Tess mentioning that the Waldrons were some of the first settlers in New York State."

Kirk smiled. At last he had found a common denominator.

"Sorry for interrupting again, Kirk."

"No problem. Believe me, I myself think it's a keen old tale. One of the locals is good friends with my aunt, and a number of years ago he gave her information about the land purchase. He also seemed to know quite a bit about the Waldron history. Garret Waldron's lineage can be traced back to a bricklayer in Albany, and then further back, to the first settlement of Manhattan which later became New York City.

"George also tells another part to the story about the inn that is quite a legend in these parts. As it happened, shortly after the inn was built, a man by the name of Evert Waldron appears in the records. We can't place him with his relationship to Garret, but suspect him to be a cousin. Before he arrived, as the story goes, he had married the beautiful Anna DuMont, who was the daughter of Henry DuMont, a French trader, and Quail's Tail, a Mohawk Indian woman. A short time after his arrival in the North Country, Evert went off to work at a lumber camp deep in the forest, and was forced to part from his wife and baby daughter. He left his family in their one-room log cabin on Waldron property. It was during this long absence that Anna was shot to death."

"Shot to death?!" Tena repeated wide-eyed.

"Yes."

"What about the baby?"

"Miraculously, their child was left unharmed, but the little one nearly died from neglect. In those times, as you can imagine, the people living in these northern mountains were far removed from the civilization of the cities, and the villages up here were quite spread out. The log homes were scattered about on the fringes of the village. It was four days before a supply wagon happened by the Waldron cabin to discover the child alongside of poor Anna's decomposing corpse."

Tena winced. "My God, how horrible!"

"A neighbor woman nursed the child back to health. Little Selene, as she was named, was barely a year old when her absent father was retrieved from the camp and returned home to view his misfortune. Anna was laid to rest beside her cabin. It is said that during her buriel, Evert went crazy with grief, fleeing to a cave in the mountains high above the creek. From what we know, he must have stayed there for weeks. That same cave, years later, became one of the main shafts of the garnet mines. Locals still call it "Evert's Cave.""

"I think I've heard of it," Tena said thoughtfully.

"Eventually he returned to care for his daughter, although he burned down the cabin and built another along the banks of the North River. When the child grew into womanhood she married Thomas Van Ness. To this day you will see many Van Ness and DuMont's listed in our local telephone book."

Tena was spellbound. "Oh, my gosh! That's Johnny's last name. I wonder if they were his ancestors? And what about Evert?"

Kirk replied thoughtfully. "He went on living a long and most prosperous life. For a number of years he remained in the North Creek area. He owned a mill and ran a highly productive farm. His enterprises produced grain for the settlers for many miles around North Creek. You know, originally our little inn was encompassed by nearly one thousand acres of choice timberlands."

"But your uncle and aunt purchased the inn from the people who built the ski complex?"

"Oh...." Kirk said softly, "then you do know a little about the Pine Cone."

"Really, I know very little."

"By the mid-eighteen hundreds the original Waldron property had been divided many times over."

Tena sighed deeply. She jumped as the Minne's horn bellowed, signaling the paddle boat's last leg of the cruise and return to Lake George's dock site.

"And so the bell tolls," Kirk stated with a twinge of disappointment. "We'll be back in fairly soon. I hate to see the night end, but it's best. You have had a hectic day, and tomorrow I have an early breakfast meeting with George and our accountant."

Walking to the forward deck, Tena said. "I still have one last question."

"What would that be?"

"Did they ever discover who killed Anna? And why?"

"That's a mystery that will forever remain undisclosed, I imagine," Kirk said. "Although, there is a story that some of the settlers came to believe that Evert himself had done the treacherous deed. Old timers used to say that Anna's beauty killed her. Rumor was that while her husband was absent she took a lover, and her husband had discovered her folly."

"Wow, that's some story!"

Kirk laughed. "It's quite a tale for sure, and, although a bit morbid, adds a little twist of interest to our marketing strategy."

Tena wrapped her sweater around her shoulders. "Morbid isn't the word – it's downright heart-rendering. How could anyone have done such a terrible thing, and then leave the infant to starve?"

"Worse yet, the child could have been eaten by wolves. Back in those times there was always a high bounty on the wolves because there were so many of them. What is more remarkable is that it was said that when they discovered the body of Anna and the baby, there were no less than a half dozen gray wolves lying in front of the open cabin door."

"That was miraculous," Tena murmered. "Of course, something else occurs to me, which I'm sure has been a topic of many conversations over the years, and that is, if Evert didn't kill his wife, then who did?"

"It's been suggested that the child was not his at all, but was the seed of the lover. But, most of these rumors and folk tales treat Evert Waldron kindly, and as far as I know few believe that he was the murderer. On the other hand, by the middle of the nineteenth century there is no record of any of the Evert Waldron family living in the area. It seems that this particular leg of the family moved to parts unknown.

"If Evert didn't do it, then all of those people in the settlement might have lived the rest of their lives with a murderer amongst themselves."

Kirk shrugged. "Who knows, but you must admit that the story is a captivating one. The narration never fails to enhance the color of our modest establishment."

Later, as they disembarked the Minne-Ha-Ha, Tena was more convinced than ever that she was receiving spiritual help from above in her quest. She also experienced a new sensation, a feeling of genuine connection to the Waldron side of herself that left her tingling with mixed emotions.

Kirk went for the car. As she stood alone near the dock, she again looked up into the deep, dark sky at the myriad of stars and the bright disk of the nearly full moon. She could not help but feel that the stars were her ancestors looking down from above, and that the bright orb, the strange and wondrous Northern Moon, was mysteriously pulling her towards her ultimate destiny.

Maybe her mother was right. God was listening to her prayers after all.

Chapter 12

George pulled his wife to the side of the dining room's plastered arched entrance. He gestured nervously toward their young female guest, who stood in front of their massive hutch admiring an array of rare antiques and seventeenth century Dutch Majolica dishes lining the shelves. It was obvious that Tena was particularly interested in the old caudle cup with the silver double handles. The couple could see that she had noticed that the cup's etched letter surrounded by ornate sketches of leafing was the initial "W". "This is bad business," he whispered to Lillian.

"Don't be so worried," Lillian whispered back.

"I am worried, Lil. This isn't right. I should have done the right thing twenty years ago and gone to that girl's mother right after Ben's funeral. After all, she is Ben's child, and now you just wait and see if all this doesn't blow up in our faces. Kirk, from what I'm hearing, has already given her a head start," George scowled. "He's always so anxious to impress the gals, one way or the other."

Lillian lifted her chin. Her smoothly defined, oval face glowed pink. Her reply was emphatically precise. "I thought that you had come past all of your reservations about Kirk. He told you he had been out with her, even though he knew you wouldn't approve, and it seemed to me that you appreciated him telling you. Otherwise, you were perfectly happy with him until she arrived."

George sighed. "Well, yes, that part is true."

"I'm sure that he only meant to recount an interesting bit of local history that any one of fifty people might have repeated to her before he did. So what if she knows who built the Pine Cone or the ancestry of the property? It's common folklore, nothing for you to be so upset over."

George shook his head. He had bags under his eyes, and his skin had taken on an ashen pallor. "Ever since that young woman walked in here last weekend, I've been thinking about Ben. It's as if he's saying to me, 'take care of this for me, Georgie.' I keep hearing him so clearly, as though he were standing right where you are now. You have to consider something, Lil; I can't forget that Ben saved my life over there. Surely, I can't forget that the man saved both our lives all over again when he loaned me the additional money I needed to buy back this piece of the old farm estate from Henderson Corporation. I would never have been able to do it on my own, even with the GI loan I obtained. What did I have in my pocket for all the repairs this place desperately needed to get us on our feet?"

Lillian fidgeted with her blouse collar. She stepped toward the hall mirror, admiring her reflection in the glass. Although nearing sixty, her dark hair, worn stylishly short, was completely free of gray. "We committed no crime, George," she sighed softly.

"My partner trusted me, Lillian. He believed we were preserving something of his dad and his granddad that would be here for posterity. When he heard that they planned to tear down Ivan's farmhouse in order to make way for the golf course, he was worried that all of this would go too, and there wouldn't be any sign that a Waldron had ever walked these parts. You know how he felt about all of that. Henderson made big promises to Ben's dad. They promised Hank that the farmhouse and this old inn would remain, but all that changed after Hank passed on. With the prospect of the farm being leveled, it was obvious that Ben could see the writing on the wall for the inn."

Lillian bolted for the kitchen, suddenly remembering she had left a pot of coffee on the stove burner. George followed, and after removing the pot she turned to her husband, "Sweetheart, all that's in the past, and Ben is gone now many, many years. That's that. This is a ridiculous conversation, George."

"I don't know about that," George snapped.

"I'm not going to argue with you about this. Excuse me while I attend to what needs doing out there."

George leaned against the kitchen countertop. His thoughts cut deep. *Ben thought that he knew me so well. Lil's right though, Ben is gone, and it's because of us the old place remains. We're the ones who have kept it going all these years, and I shouldn't let it all bother me so. Lord knows, Ben wasn't interested in running any kind of business up here, no more than he was interested in taking over the farm, which was why Hank had gone ahead and started proceedings to sell. The old man was so sick with the cancer that he lost his heart for it all, especially with his wife gone. And in the beginning, with their folks gone, the boys wanted out. Bob out west and then, after the war, Ben had had his fill of the Adirondacks. Well, who could blame him after the dirt he had been dealt.*

Her mission accomplished, Lillian returned to her husband's side. "George, I won't let you do anything foolish. Where do you think you're going to find $25,000 to give back to Miss Waldron out there? What about me, George? You know what bringing up the past would do to me. Have you lost all feeling toward me?"

"Lillian, please..."

"No, George, I insist you listen to me. Everyone in this town thinks that you married a wealthy, southern woman of blue-blooded, refined quality who brought you family funds as seed money that was invested into our business. I won't have every woman in my bridge club snooping around in my former life. I just won't have it. If you try to make amends with this young woman now, it wouldn't be long before everything comes out about my brother as well, and we would be disgraced."

"I don't want to think about James," George whispered in disgust.

"Please don't speak in that tone about my brother," Lillian pleaded.

George studied his wife patiently as Lillian made the sign of the cross over herself. "I know how you feel, Lil; that it's unchristian to speak badly about the dead, and believe me, I sincerely hope that James has found peace with his maker. I'm sorry, but times like this, I wish he'd never come up here that summer. Although, I would never have met you had it not been for James, and God knows that I am grateful for that much. It's just that I can't help but blame James for the misery we have suffered on his account," George lamented.

"No one knows, George," Lillian whispered. "Everyone is gone now that was a part of it. Please, dear, don't put worry in the middle of the street where someone is sure to trip over it. I can't see the sense to that."

George groaned. "I don't know how much longer I can live with this thing. I'm not a bad man, Lil."

"Of course not, George."

"Let me finish now, Lil. For the most part, I have tried to do the decent, right thing. I took Kirk into a partnership because I thought it would please you, and true, his investment has allowed us to make renovations that I had wanted to do for years, and having him here to cover the inn during the wintertime has worked out very well. Sometimes, however, I get the feeling that your nephew has just a little bit more of his Uncle James in his blood than is good for any of us."

Sighing deeply she said, "You're right, George. We were selfish when we kept quiet after Ben died, but now we have no choice but to remain silent. Don't you see that?"

George started toward the dining room. His anger was suffocating him, but he wasn't quite finished. He had one last concern. Facing his wife he said, "I don't know, Lil. I just don't know. It may well be that our silence won't keep this quiet for much longer. I find it disturbing that after all these years, Ava's boy has also developed an interest in his forbearers. Doesn't that strike you as odd?"

"George, please... at least think about our situation before you do anything," Lillian pleaded again.

Cupping Lillian's chin, he looked deep into her eyes. His mouth twisted as he spoke. "Ben trusted me. All we had between us, Lil, was our mutual trust and that IOU we signed in Pip's bar that afternoon – the one you burned in the fireplace the night after Ben's funeral."

Lillian lowered her eyes. Tears had begun to form as they heard Kirk's footsteps on the back steps leading into the kitchen. Seeing his distraught aunt and uncle he hesitated before entering the room, "Aunt Lillian, whatever is the matter?"

Lillian quickly composed herself, forcing a pleasant smile to her lips. "Oh, nothing at all, honey, your uncle and I were just being a couple of sentimental fools," she said glancing at George.

"That's right. Your aunt is a sensitive Sally. She gets all blubbery and gushy over nothing."

Lillian groped for a way out of her embarrassed position," Yes, I'm that way, I'm afraid. Your uncle and I were just reminiscing back to when he first bought this lovely place. I'm afraid that you'll have to forgive me, Kirk. I do get this way every year around the date that George first carried me over the threshold."

George smiled sheepishly at his wife, putting his hands in his pockets, and Kirk accepted the explanation. He knew his aunt could be quirky at times. He headed for the coffee pot, but turned on his heel after a few steps. Winking at George he said, "That's right, I almost forgot, you mentioned a wedding anniversary coming up."

"Trying to save my skin, are you?" George threw back. *Nothing about any of this would be resolved today*, he thought.

Lillian was more than a trifle anxious to change the course of their conversation and wondered just how much of what passed between her and her husband was overheard. "George was commenting on the renovations, such a big difference between then and now."

Anxiously observing his aunt, he asked, "Tears of joy, I hope?"

"Oh, Kirk, now don't get yourself into a fret. It's that George and I are so pleased with all you've done. I've written your mother and told her how happy we are that all of this has worked out. Goodness, Kirk, don't be too concerned over a few nostalgic sniffles. Women do these things, you know."

Kirk smiled, he never knew a woman who did the expected. "I would think that sentimentality ought to be a lady's prerogative," he said gently.

"Well," George said abruptly. "I've got things to do this morning, and I won't make any headway standing around, so I'll be on my way." George started toward the cellar door.

After he had gone, Kirk offered a gentle explanation, "George hasn't been himself for a week. Even our guests notice how distracted he has become."

Lillian put the coffee cups into the sink. "You know, as I say, we are delighted with everything you've done. Truly – everything, Kirk, but George has been a little worried that our valuable, antique, Dutch Majolica might be placed in a more precarious spot than is wise. After all, my collection is over three hundred years old and quite priceless. I would be devastated if something were to happen to any of it." Lillian entered the dining room with Kirk trailing her.

She nodded in Tena's direction at the far end of the room, where the young woman was still admiring the caudle cup piece from her seat at her table. Lillian whispered to Kirk, "I think that your uncle would have preferred that you left those pieces in particular in a safely secured box up in the attic loft."

"Oh," Kirk said. "I understand. He patted his aunt's shoulder, "The situation can be remedied very easily," he comforted.

"I'm glad to hear you say so," Lillian replied.

"Keep in mind that I did take out extra insurance to cover us, but if George is worried about breakage or theft, I'll call Jim Becker right away and make the arrangements for him to come over. His work is superb. He can measure for a custom curio cabinet with glass doors that we can lock securely, yet the pieces will still be viewable."

"Yes, of course, Mr. Becker is an excellent carpenter, but..."

"You tell George to rest easy, and he's not to give the matter another thought. He's right. We need to protect our precious valuables, but, of course, we wouldn't want to deny our guests the pleasure of admiring the pieces. They add so much to the ambiance of the inn." Before Lillian could further protest, Kirk slid past her and began flipping through his Rolodex on the kitchen corner desk for Jim Becker's telephone number. He picked up the receiver and dialed.

Lillian gave a subtle sigh of defeat and then decided to take another course of action.

"I've been sorely remiss with you I'm afraid," Lillian began as she approached Tena's table.

Tena could feel her face redden. Kirk must have told his aunt what she had said to him Thursday night while on the Minne-Ha-Ha. She wondered just how much of their evening he had shared with Lillian. "What do you mean?" Tena tried keeping a casual manner.

"Kirk mentioned that I might have hurt your feelings. I've been especially busy of late, but my being over-occupied at the expense of one of my guests is inexcusable, and I hope that you will forgive me," Lillian explained. Her words were soft.

"You know, Lillian, I might have been just a little bit oversensitive and should never have mentioned anything to Kirk. Anyway, if there were anything to forgive, you're forgiven."

"Good," Lillian responded. "May I sit down with you?"

"Sure, please do."

"I saw you admiring our delftware and silver serving pieces."

"I'm very taken with Americana; the plates are so pretty, and the silver, especially this two handled silver cup, is remarkable. They look very old."

"Yes," Lillian replied. "they are quite priceless. We found those rare beauties some years ago all packed away in the attic. We never displayed them publicly before my nephew arrived, but Kirk thought it would be a quaint touch. He was right, of course."

"As I said, they are lovely."

Lillian paused, measuring her words before she spoke, "Kirk tells me that he shared some of our local family history, and you believe that you are a distant descendant of Garret Waldron?"

"Oh, but, I don't know for sure about that," Tena replied uncomfortably.

Lillian smiled serenely as Mae Burns, the inn's Saturday girl, came by the table. Without a word, Mae laid down a second flowered china cup and saucer on the white lace tablecloth. She poured Lillian's cup full and refilled Tena's. Lillian folded her cloth napkin into her lap. "Thank you so much, Mae."

Tena glanced up at the server. "Thank you."

"Will you have cream?"

"Yes, thank you."

"I would have thought that you would have heard a few of the Waldron fables from somebody by now," Lillian ventured smoothly while sipping her black coffee. "There are locals who claim Anna's spirit haunts the Pine Cone."

"Not a word from anyone about any haunting," Tena said, "but, I was quite enthralled with Kirk's story of Anna and the history of the inn the other night." She paused, waiting for a reaction, but Lillian remained casual. Tena thought their conversation peculiar. *What was all of this? Why was she so interested in her now after a week of ignoring her?*

"Have you enjoyed your stay here at the inn?" Lillian persisted.

"Yes, I have." She responded honestly.

"Kirk tells me that you had a very exciting and productive week."

Tena blushed, and Lillian added hastily, "You met a brother that you never knew that you had?"

Me and my big mouth, Tena thought. "Yes, exciting is one way to describe pulling a brother out of a hat." She quickly drained the remainder of her coffee. "You know, Lillian, I've really got to be going." She stood and pushed in her chair. She had no intention of making Lillian a pal. "It's been very nice talking with you, and I hope that we get a chance to chat again."

"Yes, that would be lovely," Lillian, replied.

"I'm really sorry, but I have an appointment this morning."

This time it was Lillian's turn to blush. "Oh, I'm sorry...I didn't mean to keep you from anything. I only wanted to make my amends with you; that was all. Will you be leaving us then tomorrow?"

"Unfortunately, yes." Tena said, her heart full of mixed emotions. "The week has flown by, and I hate to go back to work, but such is the plight of the working girl."

Lillian also stood up. "Do enjoy the last of your vacation. The sun is finally coming out today, and it looks as if we are in store for another beautiful day. And, Tena, I hope that you'll come back and stay with us again sometime in the near future."

"Well, thank you, Lillian." Tena turned around, smiled, and waved as she left, feeling that she was justified telling a tiny white lie. She didn't have an appointment, but Lillian was right about the weather; it truly was going to be a gorgeous day, and the fact was that she just didn't feel like being interrogated any more today.

Chapter 13

After leaving the Pine Cone, Tena had in mind to take her time this morning and ride up to Indian Mountain Lookout Point. The night before, one of the guests had displayed an impressive array of Indian arrowheads that he and his wife had gathered on their excursion up to the Point during the week. He raved about the million dollar view, insisting that one could see for over a hundred miles from there. Tena felt that hunting for arrowheads where the treetops brushed the heavens would have been an irresistible adventure to a young boy such as Ben Waldron. She didn't want to miss it either. It would also be great to be alone with her thoughts for a little while before she met Johnny.

He had called late the previous night giving directions to the Loon Lake boat launch a few miles outside of town. They both agreed that they would rather not be two curious goldfish in the North Creek village bowl again. There were no two ways about it, that was exactly how she was beginning to feel, though it was her own fault if she did. After all, it was a small town, and she had been poking into every corner and had every pebble on every street under a microscope. People were bound to be talking or at least wondering what she was doing there.

With some time on her hands, she meandered down one of those side streets where she found three, small, handmade ceramic, flower broaches in a perky little gift shop. She couldn't resist dropping these by the nursing home where she eagerly presented her gifts to Tess, Olive, and Florence as a thank you for all the doors that they had opened for her.

Olive was consistent in her exuberance over being part of what she referred to as the "big scoop mystery of the unknown woman in the graveyard". Tess and Florence chuckled as Tena tried to tell them all once again that she worked in advertising, and not in the editorial department at the newspaper, but Olive wouldn't hear of it and had taken to calling her Nellie Bly. Tena wished that her job were one tenth as exciting as Olive seemed to think it was, but, as the visit played out, she realized that all the ladies, as well as at least one member of the nursing home staff, had become, in one way or another, participants in the Waldron family mystery. Her impromptu visit had also provided the answer to at least a portion of that mystery.

Tess had confessed that it had been she who had sent the small, silver, monogrammed spoon to her, saying that her attendant, Kelly, had mailed it for her. Apparently Tess had read in the Albany paper an article on Capitol District Women in Business, and saw her name as the recipient of the Diamond Award. Tena wasn't quite clear how on earth she had obtained her home mailing address, but would dig into that later.

Tess had also confirmed that her gift was indeed a funeral spoon, as Tena's mother had suggested. The spoon had been in her husband's family for generations. Unfortunately, the card mentioning the original owner, like so many other keepsakes, seemed to have gotten lost when Tess moved into the nursing home. But Tess did recall that the spoon marked the death of a man named Peter Waldron who she believed had lived in Albany early in the 1700's, and was a distant Waldron ancestor. She conjectured that she could remember this much because her late husband's name was also Peter Waldron. She further supposed that possibly Garret Waldron might have been at the burial, and the spoon was passed along through his descendants.

After leaving the home, Tena drove to Indian Mountain where she did indeed enjoy a spectacular view, but found no artifacts. Disappointed that she had nothing further of antiquity to hold in the palm of her hand, she had another idea. She returned to the graveyard and the marker for Garret Waldron. Kirk's account of Garret had triggered her imagination further, prompting her to want to seek out poor Anna DuMont Waldron's grave as well.

Despite the constant swatting at the swarms of seasonal pesky Adirondack black flies, she persistently searched the graveyard for over an hour, weaving throughout the slabs that covered the remains of the original pioneering settlers, but she was unable to find any reference to Anna. Finally, as had happened the day of her arrival, time ran short, she was unable to further endure the bugs, and concluded that Anna's marker must have sunk far into the ground, disappearing the way so many others had most probably done. She copied Garret's gravestone inscription onto a small writing tablet after an unsuccessful attempt at making a rubbing, an action that she knew Olive would find sinful.

Returning to the main road, she followed Johnny's directions, eventually pulling on to the dirt road leading to the boat launch. She found him leaning casually against his car, concentrating upon two fly fishermen clad in high rubber boots as they waded knee deep into the far end of the lake's cove. He didn't see her park by the tackle shack. For a moment she sat back and studied him.

Although her mother had misgivings, she was beginning to believe that this interesting man was indeed her brother. Why else would she feel so connected to him if they weren't related? Other than the color of their hair, and those Waldron dimples, the two of them bore no physical resemblance, yet almost immediately following their meeting at Garnet Manor she had felt somehow connected. She was comfortable with him, and she had the feeling that he felt the same way about her. Although she had no reason to do so, she trusted him. He appeared to be devoid of pretentiousness.

She didn't have long to scrutinize her new brother. Johnny must have sensed her presence because he turned and waved. When he approached her car, her enthusiasm for their afternoon campaign to explore the Waldron family plots heightened. As her grandmother, Honey, would have suggested, she would listen and hear the affirming song of the wood thrush whistling hope through the wind.

She rolled down the car window. "Hi there."

"Hi, Tena. You ready for all of this?"

"Absolutely. Do you think it's okay to leave my car parked here?"

"I don't see a problem. We're only going to be gone for a few hours, I figure." Johnny grinned. "Long enough for us to make an appearance before Waldron and Company up on cemetery hill, and then for me to buy you a bite of lunch as promised."

After nestling back into Johnny's Volkswagon, he turned to her, "I'm not being disrespectful to our forbearers. You know that, right?"

"I think it's safe to say that we both have their, and our, best intentions at heart."

Johnny put the key into the ignition and started the car. "So we're off." Suddenly he turned off the ignition.

"What?" Tena asked, wrinkling her nose.

"It's not in the initial plan, but how about a movie later. I mean, let's make a day of it. Who knows when we'll be able to get together again? What do you say?"

After a pause, Tena said, "Let's do that, but, what about my car?"

Johnny glanced thoughtfully at the Camero on the other side of the boat launch parking lot. "I think it will be safe enough. I'm sure a lot of folks leave them for hours at a time over there, and I'm sure too that we'll be back before it's dark."

"Lead the way then, Captain. You know, I'm all for a movie as long as it's a comedy. I could use a few good laughs. I've been feeling kind of blue, or maybe just confused is a better way to describe how I've been feeling these past weeks. All this dwelling on the past is interesting, but after we make this last, nostalgic journey, I'll be ready to join the real world again."

Johnny smiled. "I hear you."

Driving toward the cemetery, they talked about their mutual families. Tena told him about her half-sister, Kay, and how Kay's father had been killed in a company accident.

They laughed good naturedly about Olive's new role as assistant to Nellie, and discussed Jack Nicholson's role in "One Flew over the Cuckoo's Nest," Johnny jokingly saying that he thought that there had been many times in his life that he could empathize pretty well with a crazy man.

"It's not easy sometimes to determine who is sane, or what a sane person is supposed to be like," Tena ventured.

Johnny readily agreed. "If I meet someone, and they aren't just a little bit strange, I figure they just aren't healthy."

Tena nodded. "What a boring life if everybody looked, talked, and felt exactly the same. You're right; different, or strange, as you put it, is not only healthy, but also interesting. Think how many dress designers would be put in the unemployment line if they put the same thing on the cutting board every day. That would work in China...maybe, but never in America."

"You gals would be in big trouble then. But, hey," Johnny added soberly, "millions of people are walking those streets out there, and every one of them is marching to the beat of his or her own drum."

"That's for sure. There's a protest demonstration about something or other every day on the Capitol Building steps in Albany."

"So I hear," Johnny sighed, "I have a cousin who works not far from there at the State Office Building in downtown Albany. Demonstrations aren't my thing. I did two tours of Vietnam – flew a helicopter, and I was cured of freaky hair and all that stuff when I signed up."

"You...freaky hair?"

"I know it's probably hard to imagine it, but I had hair as long as yours in my senior year of high school."

Tena said, "Hair isn't an issue with me."

"So what issues might you have?"

"I've never had any use for war protesters. Not that I think being in Vietnam made any sense, it was horrible, and I'm glad it's finally ended, but burning our flag in the streets is an insult to our soldiers and really to every American. I just can't understand anybody wanting to be so unsupportive of our kids when they were over there fighting and dying."

"Neither can I, but I guess those folks figure it's their American right to speak their minds, just the same way I felt that I was entitled to my feelings about others spitting on our vets coming home. Even though it never happened to me, I remember hearing about it from some of my buddies who experienced it firsthand, and seeing it on the news as the guys made their way through airports. I'd have thrown those people in jail for a month. As for flag burning, it's my opinion that all those nuts should also be thrown into jail. I say, if you don't like it, then leave it."

Johnny drove the next few miles in silence before asking the question that, prior to their Vietnam discussion, Tena thought would come.

"Oh, heck," he said finally, "I might as well get it out in the open. There's one question I've been dying to ask. I'm wondering how it is that a real looker like you never got hitched."

Tena smiled, thinking, *You have to kiss a lot of frogs before you find Prince Charming.* She said, "I have trouble telling the good guys from the bad guys sometimes."

"Oh..." Johnny responded quietly. "That situation holds true for a lot of guys as well."

"So, do you have a girl?" Tena asked matter-of-factly.

Johnny grinned. "Yep, I have two."

"Two?"

"Two Yellow Lab's: 'Happy' and 'Sissy,'" he said pulling up to the Union Cemetery.

Tena giggled, "I see."

The two of them got out of the car and began walking up the stone driveway behind the Baptist church that fringed the cemetery. "My uncle is buried over in that section," Johnny mentioned reverently as he pointed toward the rear right end of the graveyard. "But the Waldron graves are all up there on the top of the hill by those trees. The very old ones are down here in the front."

They began climbing up the side of the steep hill toward a pair of large pines. The staunch trees appeared to be standing guard as if they were all-knowing Lords watching over their eternally silenced tenants below. The sky darkened, threatening a summer storm as the two explorers made their way between the headstones. As they approached the evergreens midway to the summit, Johnny noticed a man dressed in a sports shirt and jeans walking around the Waldron plot.

"Looks like someone else came to visit Ben and the family," he said.

Tena caught only a quick glimpse of the visitor before he disappeared behind the trees, but it was long enough to recognize George MacArthur.

Chapter 14

Kay and Tena sat across from their mother on the sweetheart swing listening to Otto and Jake debate shuffleboard game rules. The two men had already played several matches on Otto's self-poured concrete court. Tena rolled her eyes. "Do you think they're ever going to get that grille going? We need to get the coals lit. I'm starved."

"Oh, let them go," Bertha admonished leisurely. "It's still early, and our salads are made. They're winding it up."

Kay observed her mother, silver-haired, round and content to be whiling away time while enjoying one of her most prized gifts…her backyard swing. "So, Ma, what do you think about all this Waldron stuff that Tena has dug up?"

After a few moments of thought Bertha replied. "I don't know what to make of it, but Tena's adventure sure has brought back memories,"

"I knew it would," Kay responded dryly.

Bertha gazed at her younger daughter, and after a few moments thought she said, "All I know is that I haven't seen you enjoy yourself this way in such a long time. I was against you going up there, as you know, but the trips seem to have done you a lot of good. By the way, have you ever found out anything about that woman you encountered in the cemetery? You know, the one who vanished in broad daylight?"

"No, I'm still investigating," Tena responded coolly.

Kay threw a few peanuts across the yard to a grateful squirrel. "I'll tell you one thing, I'm glad she isn't going out with that Kirk anymore. I didn't trust him one bit."

Bertha said, "I didn't know that you had met him, Kay."

Tena quickly interrupted. "No, she hasn't met him, and I haven't decided not to see Kirk. I've only had a couple of dates with him, and I haven't decided anything. These days, I'm just going with the flow. Where do you get these ideas, and what gives you the right to be so damn critical of someone you've never met?"

Kay snapped back, "Well, I haven't met him, that's true, but from various conversations with you, I can figure out that this innkeeper is not the kind of man who would make you happy. Haven't you had enough jerks in your life? You deserve a break."

"Now girls, let's not fight. Talking about all of this, your aunt Jane called yesterday afternoon. Speaking of jerks, she said that she ran into Ken at the supermarket the other day."

Tena said. "I'm surprised at you, Mom, I thought you liked Ken."

"I did, but now I understand perfectly why you broke it off with him. Jane said that he had his former wife and two small children with him who were calling him Daddy. I was floored. I mean, I knew, of course, that he was divorced, but I have never heard a thing about him having children. My heavens, Precious, you know I want much more than that for you."

"I'm afraid that Ken was a whole lot less than honest," Kay said.

"What is all that about? Do you know anything about what's going on with Ken, Tena?"

Tena shrugged, tossing another peanut from the dish sitting in her sister's lap out into the yard. "I'd rather not talk about him today. What's the point."

"You know what I think, Kay?"

"No, Ma, what do you think?"

"I think you two girls had a secret, and you knew about all of this with Ken for quite some time."

Kay laughed. "No, only since Tena told me about what she had discovered. I had guessed at the possibility that Ken wasn't divorced as he had professed, and professed often, as I recall, when Tena was dating him. I suppose, Sis, that it was about a year ago that I suspected he wasn't telling us the whole truth, and that he might only be separated. But, you would only have gotten mad at me if I spoke up, so I kept quiet."

Bertha interjected, "He wasn't divorced?! I believe that I'm a little bit hurt that nobody would let me in on things."

"I was embarrassed when I found out, Mom. I would have told you eventually."

Bertha's face registered worry. "Jane said that when his supposed former wife joined her husband, and the children, he introduced Jane as an old friend. I wonder if this woman, who I now know he is married to, knew that he was dating you, Tena?"

"I wouldn't know about that, Mom."

Turning to Tena, Kay said, "I think you do know about that now."

"Kay," Bertha ordered, "if you're not going to eat those nuts, hand them over." "That squirrel is as fat as butter. Nuts are expensive."

Kay glanced over at the squirrel apologetically and ate a peanut. Addressing her mother Kay said, "She thinks this Johnny she met up north is her brother. "What do you think?"

"You know that I don't think that is true," Bertha replied quietly. "But, we've talked about all of this last week. Wishing doesn't make something so."

"Watch out, Otto, he's a sore loser," Kay called over suddenly to the men. Jake laughed good-naturedly, fluffing off his wife's catcall. "Anyway, Sis, you have a sister, and you don't need a brother."

"Thanks." Tena responded flatly. "I suppose that I should appreciate you putting on the gloves and jumping in my corner."

"You're welcome."

"You know, Kay," Bertha began reflectively, "I've often told your sister that her father wasn't a bad man. I suppose I should have put more emphasis on Ben's better traits. I was always so worried that she would pick up the drink habit. You know they say that is something that can be inherited. And then, the way he died, Tena, I just didn't want that to be a black cloud over you. I know now that I should have been more honest with you about everything."

Kay sighed. "Why do you always blame yourself?"

"That's right," Tena added.

"You were the strong one, he was the weak guy," Kay insisted.

Tena stopped the swing abruptly, joining her step-father and brother-in-law, she called back over her shoulder. "I'm sorry, I just can't do this today."

"Kay, look, now you've hurt her feelings."

"I'm sorry, Ma, but somebody has to wake her up. This sudden Waldron patronizing is more than I can take. I lived those hard times right along with you while Tena was a kid, and facts are facts. I can't go along with her trying to make Ben Waldron into a saint. He was not only a failure as a father and a husband, but he was abusive."

"Where did you ever get that idea?" Bertha asked indignantly. "Yes, he did drink, and God knows that he gave me an awful difficult time, but it wasn't weakness that kept him away from me or your sister. After his last try at the AA failed, he knew he couldn't break the habit, and I know now that he didn't want to be a drunk. He accepted our separation because he realized that he might hurt us, and it's a shame because when he was sober he was the best husband and father in the world. The way I see it, he showed a great deal of fortitude by keeping his distance. I always believed that Ben loved us very much. I know that he planned to make amends. God just took him before he could do it."

After a few minutes pondering, Kay answered, "Oh sure, like he would have carried through on that promise as he had done all the rest? Don't beat yourself up, Ma. And don't worry about Tena either. I'll give her a few minutes, and I'll go smooth her feathers. She knows that we all love her."

Bertha turned her face away, not wanting her daughter to see her pain. She recalled the first time she had laid eyes on her "Big Lug" at a company picnic baseball game. It was just her and her friend, Betty, at the start of it all; two widows raising kids alone. Sam McDermott, the shop steward at the dress factory where they worked, had coaxed them to go. Bertha smiled to herself thinking of Sam and how he was always looking out for "his girls." She could hear him as clearly as if it were yesterday, telling them that some of the guys from the factory packing department had formed a new team and were playing against the "Railroad Steamers". They called themselves the "Batting Boxers". "What you two gals need is a husband," Sam had insisted. "It sure would be a good thing if someone would come along and get you both out of my hair." So, they had gone, and she met Ben, who introduced Betty to her Stan, and life turned another corner for all of them.

"I'm sorry, Ma, I didn't mean to hurt you. I really felt bad about what happened to Ben. Remember how he liked to play that trumpet?" she asked, trying to take back the gloomy mood that she had invoked. "He was pretty good at it too."

Bertha smiled wanly. "I remember. I remember it all, even after all of these years. Much of what comes to mind I wouldn't want to relive, but Ben and I had our good moments. It's too bad that the good times were so few and far between. Just the same, I'm not sorry for the years I spent with him, any more than I would want to have missed the happiness that I have found with your father or Otto." Looking toward Tena, Otto, and Jake, she said, "I thank God everyday for everyone He has brought into my life."

After a moment of silence Kay said, "What if Johnny Van Ness isn't Tena's brother as you seem to think? Suppose something more than a platonic friendship is brewing here? Suppose that the two of them get together? I know that it's far fetched, but just suppose they do? How would you feel about that?"

Bertha shrugged. "I can't go through life worrying about every 'what if this' or 'what if that' because I can tell you that kind of thinking gets you nowhere. You know, Kay, you're beginning to sound like a yenta, scratching off names of possible suitors. We both want Tena to be happy. We can't pick our children's mates, as you well know. Jennifer will make her way in life, just as you did, and just as Tena is trying to do now. God only loans us our children for a short time, and after that we must hope and pray for the best. Anyway, as far as your sister is concerned, I have faith that God is watching over her."

Kay relented. "I guess you're right. Did you know she's meeting Johnny later today in Albany?" Getting off the swing she picked up an empty plastic pitcher from the picnic table. "I'm going in to make more iced tea. From the look of those two, and this sky, we're going to be sitting in the backyard bleachers until the washout."

"Okay," Bertha called after her, "but, we've got to get these guys moving. We may have to eat inside, but I'm not boiling those franks."

Tena looked at her watch. Turning toward Otto, she said, "Where's the lighter fluid?"

Chapter 15

A job argument with one of the site bosses coupled with heavy traffic through torrential rainfall had Johnny Van Ness running late today. On top of everything else, Albany was a frantic mess this steamy afternoon as thousands of motorcyclist demonstrators drawn from various parts of New York State crammed State Street around the Capitol Building to protest the newly implemented, and highly detested, helmet law. If he didn't have to meet their newly hired salesman at the Harrison project bid opening in downtown Albany, he would have avoided the mess and be meeting Tena on schedule. By the time he had reached the Gateway Diner's parking lot, it was full, and he ended up parking next door in the Standard Furniture lot. All of this had left him feeling damn frustrated, but it didn't matter. The world could be blowing up. He had to be here and straighten things out.

Soaked through to the skin, sneakers squeaking, Johnny pushed open the diner's glass swing door, immediately searching booths. He glanced at the wall clock and winced – he was over a half-hour late. He wouldn't blame Tena if she had given up on him, but... trailing the diamond patterned floor past a skirmish of waitresses, he saw her waving, noticing right away her bright yellow headband and great Pollyanna - Ann Margaret face. It was hard to imagine that nearly two months had passed since they had met at Garnet Manor, and what a great two months it had been. He had no reservations – none. She was it.

"You look like a drowned rat, but a cute one."

"I apologize. It's just nuts out there."

"I know. I was caught in some of it myself."

"I hope then that you weren't waiting too long."

"Ten minutes, maybe."

Tena pulled a pile of napkins from the dispenser and handed them to him to wipe the dripping rainwater from his face. As he sat down across from her, sliding along the vinyl seat, she bubbled over with her normal, melodious laughter, the gnawing memory of which regularly interrupted his sleep. Win, lose, or draw, he was especially grateful that she had made him a part of her life.

"I shouldn't laugh at you. You look like you have had an extremely rough day."

"Just the usual scurry of a rodent's life."

"I'm all ears. As Cindy would say, tell me your story."

Johnny looked at her squarely, in one flash recalling their super get-togethers over the last months: the day that they went to New York City to see the stage production, Barnum, the picnic at her sister Kay's place and the beach parties at his business partner's Lake George camp. These all crowded his mind, as did remembering the lump in his throat that occurred every time she talked about Kirk.

Returning to reality he began, "Tena, I've got one heck of a story to tell you this time. I hope you'll understand."

"I know all about it. Central Avenue was grid locked near Lark Street for twenty minutes while the cops were trying to deal with a bunch of unhappy bikers mulling around. There were a couple of cars pulled over to the curb with their windshields bashed in. I think that there might have been some arrests."

"That's not exactly what I wanted to tell you, but, you're right – it was quite a scene. Somehow I think being arrested will make them all very happy. They'll have their faces on the six o'clock news. What a deal."

"They're demonstrating about the new helmet law," Tena commented.

"Yes, I know, that's what I mean."

"I heard on the car radio that before the weekend is over they expect to see five thousand bikers here," she said.

"I'll bet that there are two thousand down there in town right now. Rain doesn't deter them."

Tena laughed, "Well, when you're on a crusade, you just ride it through; no pun intended."

"Ride it all the way through is the only way," Johnny remarked thoughtfully.

Indifferently, the waitress dropped two large laminated menus on the Formica top in front of them, hastily raced through six daily specials, and then promised to return in five minutes for their order.

"She has an attitude like a guy I knew in the Service," Johnny whispered after the girl left their table. "Kind of looks like him too."

After a fleeting look at the woman, Tena tried to suppress a giggle.

"Anyway, seriously, I'm glad we both made it."

Tena pulled out a few more napkins and handed them to him. "Why wouldn't I wait?" she retorted cutely. "I took a half-day off from work just so I could get over here by one, and after all, you bribed me. You said you were buying. How could I refuse a free lunch with my handsome brother?"

"I am buying. A date's a date," Johnny said stoically. He searched the menu. *I'm not going where I want to be*, he thought.

"Date?" The word rolled off her lips. She didn't take her eyes from the printed lunch options in her hands.

"Tena, put down your menu. I have something important that I want to tell you," he said nervously.

"Okay…"Tena said, leaning back against the booth. She locked her eyes onto his. "What's wrong? You haven't robbed a bank or something. Have you?"

He met her amused gaze head on. "Nothing is wrong, but depending on how things go, something could be very right. In fact, something could be right for the first time in a long time."

Tena gave him a quizzical look and was about to open her mouth to speak just as the waitress reappeared at the table. "What'll ya have, Hon?" she bubbled.

Johnny shot her an annoyed look that was ignored. "I don't think that we have had a chance to decide."

The waitress put her hand on her hip. "Sir, I don't wanta be pushy, but if you don't order, I can't guarantee when you'll get it. Do ya see this place? The kitchen is swamped."

"I'll just have a cheeseburger and a Coke," Tena said flatly.

Johnny sighed. "I guess I'll have the same."

"Good choice."

Tena watched her disappear with the folded menus under her arms. " 'Good choice'? Good grief, she should look for a different job."

"Right," Johnny said, but he was anxious to spit out his story before he got cold feet. He wished that he had known the truth all along, although his mother's silence and his ignorance had enabled him to meet, as well as get to know, this beautiful young woman sitting in front of him. He wouldn't waste any more time second-guessing his mother's motives for covering up a foolish youthful mistake. It was possible that she had intended to tell him someday, but then the accident happened, and that someday had never come. Paul, however, had taught him to follow his heart, and now his heart told him that it was time to get everything out in the open.

Tena wiggled on her bench seat. "Go ahead," she encouraged. "The suspense is killing me."

"All right, here goes," Johnny said. "We've talked a lot, but I never told you much about my family history, other than you know that Paul Van Ness married my mom when I was very young. He adopted me when I was four. I called him Dad, and honestly I never thought about being anyone else's kid. I was on the Little League team that Dad coached, and I played ice hockey because my dad had played when he was a kid. Mom never missed a game. We used to camp at Loon Lake every summer, and Mom used to cook the bass that Dad and I caught. They were happy times."

"Sounds like you had a nice family and a wonderful childhood."

"They are good memories," Johnny continued slowly. "Then one day while they were driving up to Montreal for a convention for my dad's work, they were killed in a car crash."

Tena could see Johnny's strong jaw tighten. She reached over and gently touched his arm. "I'm sorry. I know how it is to lose somebody you love, but an accident… and you were so young. That must have been so terrible for you."

Johnny cleared his throat. "I had bad dreams for years after, but as time went by life got better, and my Aunt Bev and Uncle Joe, who had taken me in, made a new life for me in their family. In fact Bev and I bonded together right away because I had lost my mother, and Bev had lost her only sister."

"Sounds like Bev is a very special lady."

"That she is. Bev and Joe have four girls who are real pistols, and they latched onto their moody orphaned cousin like bees to a honey pot."

"I guess they found a neat brother. I can relate to that."

Johnny straightened in his seat.

Viewing him curiously, Tena said, "Oh, no…there's that screwed up look on your face again, Van Ness. You don't have to tell me all these painful details. I don't want to hear anything that might cause you grief. You know if…"

Johnny held up his hand, stopping her in mid-sentence. "At one time I couldn't think about Mom or Dad without suffering, but now when I think of them I usually remember the laughter and the love we had for each other."

Tena smiled. "I'm glad," she said. "But then, what's going on? I can see that you're leading up to something."

"There are things that you need to know so that you'll understand my perspective," he said rubbing his eyes. What I'm getting at is that although I was hit with a big tragedy, I had a good childhood, as you just said. More importantly, I didn't know anything about Ben Waldron until I was thirteen."

"You didn't know?"

"No...nothing. Dad and Mom told me one Sunday afternoon after church that I was adopted by Paul and that my real name was Waldron. Of course, I took it like any dumb young teenager would, screaming out my miserable rage and running out of the room. I really didn't want to hear that stuff. Who would? But, I imagine that they had decided to tell me before somebody else did, and now I know that they planned to tell me a lot more, but held off."

"And when you heard that Paul wasn't your dad weren't you just a little curious?"

"In retrospect...sure, I was curious, but, as weird as it sounds now, I didn't want to hear anything. As I said before, we were the three musketeers. All of a sudden I felt like I wasn't a part of my own family.

"I haven't a foggy notion of what my mother's reasoning was back then, but she did take me up to North Creek to visit Tess that one summer. I'm afraid that I was a little hostile inside, but on the outside I was polite. Mom wouldn't stand for a fresh kid for long.

"The way I saw it, I was a Van Ness, not a Waldron. I kept telling her that all the way home, and I guess she must have gotten the message because we only went the one time.

"After the accident, I didn't come back up north until my Uncle Buck died, and only while in town for the funeral did I begin to get the urge to find out what I could about the Waldrons. That's about when my crazy dreams started."

"What kind of dreams?"

"Oh, I don't know. Wacky images that made no sense at all."

Tena leaned forward. "Guess what, I have weird dreams too."

Johnny said. "I think sometimes there is something that leads me." He hesitated while waiting for a reaction. "Far out, right?"

Tena shrugged. She had learned to be careful about taking this kind of bait. "I do believe we all have a guardian angel."

"You think you have a guardian angel?"

"Sure do and I think you have one, too."

"I don't know about angels," Johnny said. "I'm not much of a religious man. After I went to live with my relatives, well, Bev and Joe never were much for going to church.

"Anyway, I usually go by what I feel inside my gut, but you could be right. An angel on my shoulder wouldn't be so bad. Sure, I could go with that idea. Could be even a gruff guy like me could have one."

Tena reflected, "You've seen the framed needlepoint that hangs in my mother's dining room? I pointed it out to you when Mom had you to dinner two weeks ago."

"Yes, I think I do remember, something to do with the poet, Rudyard Kipling, isn't it?"

"The title of the poem is, "IF" and I think about a couple of lines quite often.

"If you can dream – and not make dreams your master;
If you can think – and not make thoughts your aim."

"Mr. Kipling must have been a wise man."

"Obviously, my mother thinks so too. She never encouraged a whole lot of daydreaming in our household. She believes in angels, but doesn't hold much with hearing voices. She puts that sort of thing down to women's intuition. Hearing voices is definitely not something to be dwelled upon in my mother's company."

Johnny smiled. "It had to be male intuition that sent me to see Tess after Buck's funeral and to hold onto that relationship."

"Male intuition?"

"Sure, without that there wouldn't have been her big surprise meeting between us," he said. "Some surprise. I was the one astonished. You see, all my life I've been searching for a girl just like you, Tena. But the big joke was on me. I mean there was the woman of my dreams, but she was my sister. 'What a bummer,' I thought. But, I'll bet Tess's treat worked for you."

"Oh, you're so sweet to say that. Yes, I thought her little dinner party was a total success," Tena said softly.

"I knew you were coming to the Manor to meet me that day," Johnny said gauging his words, "but I was the one surprised when I saw you because I never expected that such a knockout could be related to me."

Tena could feel her face flushing. "Well, I never thought of myself as a knockout, far from it," she stammered. "And, why do you think that way about yourself. I mean you're the knockout."

"No, I'm not. I'm just a regular guy, but you... you're really something special; a lady who is both fun and intelligent...a guy could go bananas for you."

"You're embarrassing me, Van Ness."

"Bear with me, I know I'm rambling, but I'll soon make my point and please don't take any offense. I mean to be complimentary; I think that you must know by now that I'm no smoothie."

"I'm your sister, not just a girl, and besides I think that you're attractive too. As you should know by now, I don't think much of smoothies."

"Yeah, well, it's the sister and the brother part that I'm here to talk about today," he said gravely.

"What do you mean?" Tena suddenly had that sinking feeling in the pit of her stomach.

Johnny paused awkwardly as their waitress shoved their orders in front of them. "You're all set then?" she asked.

"Yep, all set," Johnny said flashing a broad smile at their impatient server. She left, and he pushed his plate to the side, folding his hands in front of him on the table. "It's best if I just lay what's on my mind out in front of you. I'd love to be your brother, Tena, but I'm not."

Tena was stunned speechless. She heard her mother's words. *Ben never believed that child was his own.*

"How do you know this for sure?" she asked quietly.

"Aunt Bev told me the whole story last week. She heard me talking about you to Darlene, one of her girls."

"Stop this right now. You must be my brother. Look how similar our hair and skin tones are. Some things a person just knows – like we both like mashed potatoes and gravy. I know that sounds stupid, but I know that you know what I mean."

Johnny shook his head. "You only want it to be true; a loyalty that warms my heart, believe me," he said. "I'm disappointed, but I don't care. I mean, I really do care," his voice cracked.

Tena twisted her straw around in her soda. "What does this mean? I don't want to lose touch, Johnny. If we aren't brother and sister, I'd still like us to remain friends no matter what the future brings, if that's okay with you. Maybe we're not blood related, but you have to admit that there's definitely something that connects us together." Tena looked down into her glass whispering, "Something seems, I don't know, joyous between us every time we're together. To be perfectly honest, that flicker always embarrassed me."

Johnny reached for her hand looking into her Pollyanna face, "You really feel that way?"

"Yes, I do."

"Do you want me to finish telling you what I know?" he asked.

"You're not answering me, Van Ness. Are we going to stay friends?" Her lips trembled.

"Tena, I feel exactly as you do. When I came today I was afraid to tell you because I thought that if you knew that I wasn't your brother, I'd never see you again. I figured that you were so bent on finding out about your real father, who's been dead for twenty years, that discovering a real live brother along the way was even better for you.

"But, I'll tell you without any hesitation that if I had to make a choice between being your brother or not, I'd rather not be your brother. I hope that I'm not confusing you. I'm not good talking about stuff like this. It's just that I'm so glad that it's all out, and you feel the same way that I do."

Tena felt like a soaring eagle skimming the tops of the tallest pines of the Adirondacks. "Okay, Van Ness, tell me what you know, but I want you to take a few bites of your burger first."

Johnny willingly obeyed. He was relieved and hungry. Minutes later he pushed his half finished plate of food aside, once again anxious to share Bev's revelations. "Apparently my real name should have been Johnny La Rose. That would be meaningless to you, but I'm sure that you recognize the name Lillian MacArthur."

"So who is La Rose?" Tena asked.

"James La Rose was Lillian MacArthur's brother. The lady who runs the Pine Cone Inn is my Aunt, though I doubt that she would welcome me as her nephew. My biological father, James, came up from the south to work at Lake George one summer during the early forties when he was about eighteen years old, and he stayed. James wasn't drafted into the service according to Bev because he was partially blinded in one eye from an accident when he was a kid.

Ben Waldron had been gone a couple of years overseas, and my aunt Bev told me that my mother believed that he was dead because she didn't hear from him for over a year. Bev said that none of my mother's letters were being answered, and then finally one of his buddies had written to my mother from a hospital over there saying that he thought Ben had been killed in action.

So here was my mom, a lonely twenty-two year-old when she fell for James, who according to my aunt Bev, was a handsome dude. I know it wasn't right what my mother did, but good people sometimes make bad calls. You know what I mean?"

"Yes, I sure do," Tena said softly.

"A short time later Ben came home and my mother thought she was seeing a ghost at first. She was pretty mixed up, as anybody would be faced with a situation like that one. She and Ben went back together for a while, but my mother had already confessed to my aunt that she suspected that she was pregnant by James. My mother told my aunt that it didn't matter that she knew she still loved Ben as soon as she saw him. She had given into her loneliness and made a costly mistake. She was sure that if her husband knew the truth he could never forgive her."

Tena sat mesmerized. "Holy crow," she whispered.

Johnny said, "When Ben returned, James took off in a hurry back to Virginia. Years later they found out that he was living in New Orleans. As far as I know he never married, and Bev said that she heard that he died five years ago."

Tena interjected, "So your mother didn't go off with James La Rose?"

"No, according to Bev she was ashamed of having become involved with him, and knowing my mother, I'm sure that was true. But, she and Ben could never really get back together, although she said they tried; too much had happened between them, and the war had affected him badly; he was moody and had horrible dreams. So after a few months they separated. From what I can put together, she was staying with a married girlfriend when I was born."

"And what about Paul?" Tena asked.

"My mother knew Paul from High School. My Uncle Buck, Paul's brother, used to pal around with Ben and Bob Waldron – everybody knows everybody in a small town like North Creek. They must have stayed in touch because, much later on, after leaving your dad and with me a toddler, he and my mother finally hooked up."

"How sad for all of them," Tena said, genuinely thinking, *I thought my own love life was messed up.*

"My heart breaks to think of Mom carrying me inside of her and running away from her home town to have her baby all alone. She went to Kingston, which is the town listed on my birth certificate. The name on my original birth certificate is Waldron, but was officially changed when I was adopted. I was about two when Paul and Mom ran into each other again. He made his living building tract houses in the Kingston area back in those days. Bev and my uncle moved to Weavertown four years ago with the girls. You know the rest."

Tena tried digesting this and said, "If Lillian is your Aunt, then Kirk Morehouse is your cousin?"

"I guess he is, but who needs him? I would prefer that nobody is aware of that fact."

"Kirk is okay," Tena said. "He's a little much, but he's okay."

"Kirk is NOT a stand up guy," Johnny said stiffly.

Tena sighed. "Kirk....we don't always get to pick our relatives, do we?"

Johnny absently played with his spoon. He didn't mention that he knew Kirk had been chasing Barb Baker, a sweet nineteen-year-old friend of his cousin, Darlene, and then there was the married waitress he had heard rumors about. "I apologize for talking so foul about a relative or anyone for that matter. I didn't come here today to discuss Kirk."

"You're forgiven."

"The thing is Tena, I'm not a Waldron, and I sure don't feel like a La Rose either. I'm sure not going out of my way to embrace Kirk as a relative. Still, I do want to be a good friend to Tena Waldron. So, since I'm no longer your brother, can I take you out? eh..., you know what I mean, as an official date?"

Tena knew no deliberation was necessary. She glanced out the window. The rain had stopped. "I think that could be managed."

"So what do you say, can we start fresh this weekend? How about Istria's Steak House on Saturday night, and Sunday it just so happens that I've got two tickets...good seats.... at the Saratoga Performing Arts Center?"

Tena picked up her uneaten cheeseburger. "You've got yourself an official date, Van Ness."

Chapter 16

Tena punched her personal code into the keypad at the back employee entrance while juggling an armful of ad proofs, several of which were marked with bright red ink for copy changes. She yanked open the steel door. With no time to think about anything else but deadlines, her irritation mounted. She had to get everything into composing, pronto, and then beg Art Moyer to have his people return the revised proofs before noon so that she could check them. It was an impossible situation that she had to make doable. Budget cuts last spring had eliminated the last of the proofreaders, a sore loss endured by all. She had to double check each of her client's ads for accuracy again before allowing anything to go to final print.

Thank God for Art.

Taking a long, deep breath, she tried hard to assimilate what she had learned in stress reduction class. *Focus on something other than this, she thought. Draw in the positive; throw out the negative.* The lump in her throat began to disperse recalling Johnny's 'take it as it comes' philosophy about business.

"Walt and I build the best commercial properties in upstate New York," he told her proudly. "We build our business on referrals, but there's always that one percent who we're not going to satisfy. This drives Walt, who's a typical type A personality guy, crazy, but I always say to him that those customers weren't happy folks before they signed our contract either."

Last weekend when she complained about the uniqueness of the heinous media deadlines, Johnny had burst into laughter. "Deadlines!" he extolled. "You don't know the meaning until you have looked into the raw, wild eyes of a building owner whose building can't open for rental because the elevator doors haven't arrived. I have zero control over the elevator manufacturer, but that building owner doesn't want to hear that. Your customers or mine are all pretty much the same. That's why I took up golf. Hitting those balls does me a world of good."

Johnny and her mother shared the same attitude. Bertha insisted that someday she would look back on all of these little "bits and pieces of life" and laugh. Tena doubted that the day would come when clients like burley Bill Fergerson, the Liddo Exotic Club public relations man, or Santos, the demanding manager of Carey's Restaurant, would strike her as funny. But, she was trying to learn to put it all into perspective. She and Cindy had decided to try to lose some weight, and her mother had talked them into joining the newly organized women's basketball team at the community college.

Tena flew down the hallway past Jim McKinney who was already busy in paste up. "Morning, Jim."

"Hey, Tena. So what do you think, another day, another dollar?"

"Let's hope," Tena tossed back.

Where would I be if all my people decided to leave advertising all together? I'd be in the fast lane to the unemployment office, that's where. Mike Harrow's opening for this week's sales meeting was right on target: "Nothing happens until somebody sells something." He always added, "And remember, you need a customer to make a sale. So let's get out there and, sell, sell, sell." Mike thought the first half of this slogan important enough to tape it to the telephone receiver of everyone in the sales department.

This morning the department was unusually quiet as she dropped the bundle of work onto her desk. She noticed Mike and his new assistant hovering over the morning's paper.

As Tena entered the sales office the two glanced up, their eyes following her to her desk. Mike whispered something to his assistant who grimaced. He had that grave, serious boss expression on his face that usually meant that he had just hung up a call from an irate client, who, having noticed the incorrect copy, now refused to pay for the advertisement.

What's blowing up now?

"Hello," Mike called over to her. His voice was definitely strained. "Did you see the paper this morning?"

Tena loosened her briefcase shoulder strap and threw the battered leather bag on top of the pile in front of her. Annoyed, she glared at Mike.

Their publisher had an Eleventh Commandment: Thou Shalt Read 'Our Paper' every morning, seven days a week, beginning to end, before the wheels of progress (and of revenue) can begin to turn again.

The revenue had to roll, and as usual, in keeping to the plan, a copy of 'The Daily Record' had been deposited at everyone's station at 5 A.M. Mike's job was to enforce company policy, and he loved to bust chops the minute anyone came in the office. He usually had ready his "newsworthy question" to throw in every lap as soon as he or she sat. Of course, she understood the logic of knowing one's product before trying to sell it, but this morning she wasn't in the mood to be quizzed.

"Mike, give me a break, will you!" she whined back.

The new assistant scurried away headed for the hallway that led to the cafeteria door, "See ya," she called over her shoulder to Mike.

Mike, coffee cup in hand, walked over. "I can see that you're not a happy camper today," he said.

"No you're wrong. I'm just busy, Mike."

"Have you seen the paper?"

"No, I haven't seen it yet." Tena could hear the strain in her voice.

"Rest easy, Kiddo, I don't have any zingers for you this morning, but I would suggest that you take a look at the paper before you hit the bricks again today."

"Come on, now, I always read it, Mike. I'd just like to get my stuff organized first. I've got to get all of this in ASAP."

"Sure, I know you do," Mike retorted, putting down his cup and taking the bunched layouts from her that she had just retrieved out of her in-box. "We'll get it all in, don't worry. Tena, I want you to read the paper. Read the header, and then take it from there," he ordered as he piled her work on the corner of the desk. He reached for the coffee, draining down the last of it.

Tena began to read the newspaper's headline out loud as Mike watched her face. ***"DOUBLE MURDER AND SUICIDE IN LAKE GEORGE"***

"Read further, Tena. Check out the victims," he urged.

Tena's eyes followed down the editorial column.

Lake George, New York, September 26th,

by Joe Bennett

Three local Adirondack Mountain residents met violent deaths last night while at a trendy Lake George hot spot in what appears to be a crime of passion. Elizabeth (Betty) Cobb, a lifelong resident of the village of Lake George, who was employed as a waitress at the Bo Jam Bo's Restaurant and Lounge, a popular gathering place for tourists and locals alike, was shot in the head at point blank range allegedly by her husband, John Paul Cobb, also of Lake George, N.Y. John Blake, the coroner at the scene, said that Mrs. Cobb died instantly.

Mr. Kirk Morehouse, of North Creek, N.Y., was also a victim of this shooting. He was pronounced dead upon arrival at Saratoga Hospital.

According to a witness, a Mr. Murray Rapt, who tends bar at Bo Jam Bo's evenings, Mr. Cobb appeared to be under the influence of alcohol when he entered the establishment and threatened to kill everyone in the place. There were several other patrons present at the time of the crime, and Mr. Rapt told this reporter that he didn't doubt for one minute that John Cobb meant business, saying, "He had that look in his eyes."

Witnesses said Cobb had caused previous trouble at Bo Jam Bo's during the summer, and had had to be escorted from the premises. On another occasion two weeks previous, he reportedly came into the club calling his wife obscene names and disturbing the other customers. Mr. Rapt said that Cobb had been asked to leave and had complied.

Another eyewitness, Angela Benson, a co-worker of Mrs. Cobb, said she was only a few feet from Betty Cobb when her husband entered the room. She also told this reporter that she heard Mrs. Cobb whisper to Mr. Morehouse, "Watch out! I'm afraid he's got a gun." Witnesses relate that at this point Mr. Cobb turned directly towards his wife, mumbled something, pulled out his gun, and then fired at his wife. Mrs. Cobb fell to the floor and didn't move.

Miss Benson said that Mrs. Cobb had confessed to her only a few days before that her husband had threatened to kill her if she ever tried to leave him. Mrs. Cobb had also confided to Miss Benson that her husband had accused her of being unfaithful in their marriage.

"Her husband was crazy, rest assured that Betty never did anything except talk to the guy. She was flattered by Kirk Morehouse's attention, that's all," Miss Benson said. Miss Benson, who had been close friends with the deceased, was later escorted home by police officers.

According to Mr. Rapt, after Mr. Cobb shot his wife, the enraged perpetrator then turned viciously on Mr. Morehouse, a part owner of the Pine Cone Inn located in North Creek and a frequent customer at the lounge on Thursday evenings.

According to Rapt, Mrs. Cobb was sitting with Mr. Morehouse while on break when her husband burst in. After Mr. Cobb shot his wife, he shouted vulgarities at Morehouse and then proceeded to fire three shots into him while Rapt himself stood in terror behind the bar. "God help me, I saw it all. He yelled at me to stay put or I'd get it too, and I took him at his word," Rapt said.

The first shot, according to Rapt, entered his second victim's lower abdomen, and the wounded Kirk Morehouse doubled over. Mr. Cobb laughed at Morehouse as he pleaded for his life, and placed the barrel of his gun directly against the man's right temple, firing a second shot. Cobb fired the third, and final shot, into Morehouse's chest as he lay motionless a few feet from Cobb's wife.

According to Mr. Rapt, for a moment Cobb had stood silently over the two corpses, holding the gun by his side, but, after muttering something that Mr. Rapt took to be, "it's over," he put his gun to his head and discharged his weapon one final time.

Other terrified witnesses at the scene stated that Mr. Cobb came into the lounge at Bo Jam Bo's at approximately 8 P.M. Sid Zimbrousky, the restaurant's dining room manager, noted that Betty Cobb usually ended her shift at eleven o'clock, but she had been visibly upset in the kitchen, and he told her to take an early break. Not long after, he saw her take two cups of coffee to a table in the lounge where she and Kirk Morehouse then talked for perhaps five minutes or so before her husband entered the room. "It all happened so fast, nobody could have stopped him," Zimbrousky added.

Upon further extensive questioning of all those who had been present at the time of the shootings, several other witnesses reported hearing Mr. Cobb saying to his wife and Mr. Morehouse just before he pulled out his gun, "You're both done."

Mike could see Tena shaking while she stood and continued to read the accounting of the previous night's brutal events. He swung around her chair.

"Here, you need to sit down," he insisted.

Tena sank into her seat, fearing that she was about to be sick to her stomach.

"I saw Kirk two weeks ago," she mumbled. "We met over at Skippy's on Lark Street for coffee."

Mike squeezed her arm compassionately. "I thought that this Kirk Morehouse person was the same one that you had met while vacationing up North during the summer," he whispered.

Tena's head was reeling. She felt dizzy.

"Now, take it easy," Mike said, pulling up another chair.

"This is such a shock."

"I can see that."

"He never gave me any indication that he was going with anyone else, but of course, it would be silly to think that a good looking man like Kirk wouldn't be dating. I mean he had the right to date, but I can't imagine that he would be mixed up with a married woman."

Mike sighed deeply. "You weren't still involved with him were you?"

Tena felt her face flush. "You mean, was I sleeping with Kirk Morehouse?" she stammered briskly. "Not that it's any of your business, Mike, but no, I wasn't sleeping with him. Actually, it's not my style to pick up guys on a vacation."

"Look, I didn't mean..."

"Whatever might have been with him was really over before it got started. But, I did consider Kirk a friend. It's horrible to know that he's been butchered." Tears began to well up in her eyes.

Mike stiffened, obviously embarrassed. "You're so right. I have no place questioning you like this. I don't know where my head is this morning."

Tena mumbled, "This is just insane."

"Why don't you take the rest of the day off," Mike suggested gently. "I'll put your ads into the composing room for you, and have somebody proofread the revisions. That way you won't have to be answering any more dumb questions, and you'll have the weekend to recover from the shock of all of this. We all mean well enough, Tena, but they're bound to be curious. Not that there was anything serious, of course, but everybody knew that Morehouse was an acquaintance of yours."

Nodding, she numbly picked up her car keys that she had thrown what felt like a lifetime ago on the desk. "Sorry I bit your head off Mike. Thanks for being concerned."

"It's okay," Mike replied.

She was in a complete daze as she left the office, her head full of a jumble of feelings and flashbacks of Kirk and her trips north. Even when she reached her car her hands continued to shake. As she turned the key in the ignition she paused to pray for Kirk's immortal soul, and for the Cobbs'.

Chapter 17

Back at her apartment, Tena moped around, her head pounding. Three days before the murders she had picked up a very disturbing registered letter from the Post Office. It had come from George MacArthur and was accompanied by a certified check made payable to her in the amount of $25,000! Briefly put, George said that the enclosed check was funds owed to her for her share in the inn, an announcement she didn't understand at all.

When she had tried to contact George, Lillian had answered the telephone. She asked Lillian if she could speak with her husband, explaining to her that she had discovered something about her father's old high school that she wanted to question George about. She carefully made no mention of the check.

Lillian had coolly informed her that George was in California on business until Saturday, and she had gotten the distinct impression that Lillian had no idea about the check that now rested in the upper drawer of her bureau.

When she was unable to contact George, she had called Kirk on Wednesday afternoon, remembering that Lillian met with her ladies club on Wednesdays. She planned to ask him a few discrete questions that she believed might shed some light on the reasons for the check. Rather than talk on the phone, Kirk had suggested a meeting at Smith's Restaurant in North Creek, adding that he also had many things that he wanted to talk over that were too involved for the phone, once again mentioning making "amends". She supposed he had meant something along the line of an apology for his behavior the night that they had sandwiches at Skippy's when she told him that she couldn't see him anymore. Although they had never been intimate, it was better that they not date. She wanted harmony between them, but clearly, Kirk didn't see it that way, and they had parted badly. She wasn't comfortable with meeting him again face to face, especially in North Creek, but had replied that she thought Smith's was too far for a work night drive, suggesting instead that they meet at Bo Jam Bo's in Lake George, which would cut her drive considerably. Kirk had agreed, and they were to have met Thursday evening at about 7:30. As she had sat in the newspaper parking lot, a chill went up her spine. That was about the same time as the murders! Another chill had gone up her spine when she remembered why she had not followed through on her meeting plans with Kirk.

Wednesday night she had slept fitfully, tossing and turning, her mind a cluttered web of turbulent dreams. Shortly after midnight she had awoken with a start, sure she had heard a persistent voice saying, "Don't go! Don't go!" The moon's light streamed through the window's sheers, casting long dim shadows everywhere throughout her bedroom. She sat up in bed feeling queasy, overwhelmed by a feeling of ominous dread; the voice, fainter now, but still undeniable, whispered slowly one last time, "Don't go!"

The next morning she had called the Pine Cone. Fortunately, Kirk had answered. She told him that she couldn't meet him now; it would have to wait. She used work as an excuse. He sounded disappointed, but said he understood. They would reschedule in a week or so. That was the last she had spoken with him.

She hadn't lied to Mike. Any close relationship that might have been with Kirk ended some time ago, but she had to admit to herself that she had been extremely attracted to him in the beginning. It was just that she could never get comfortable with Kirk, always feeling that there was a hidden side to him, something that left her on edge when she was with him. After a few dates during the summer she realized that Kirk wasn't for her.

Thinking back, the initial thrill had begun to fade soon after their moonlit cruise, and disappeared when she figured out that she was falling in love with Johnny. She had no intention of making the same mistakes that she had made in the past. She had hoped to make a friendly ending at Skippy's. However, their last minutes together had been miserable, and now she was sick at heart that the "amends" had never happened.

She found herself wondering how many other women who were acquainted with Kirk had been sharing a seat in his love boat. She felt sorry for Betty Cobb. Perhaps, she too had tried to put an end to their friendship as they had sat together that terrible last night.

Tena was beginning to see into the complexities of Kirk Morehouse, on one hand a delightfully charming, clever business man, on the other, a shallow human being who repeatedly played a vicious game with women. He paid the ultimate price. She thought poignantly, *I was willing to partake in those games once upon a time.*

Her deepest inner voice said, *be grateful that God has protected you.*

She recalled how Kirk had looked at her that night when they had stood watching shooting stars from the deck of the Minne-Ha-Ha. He had lifted her up when she was down. He had provided something when she was empty. She thought of him reclining in Lillian's red and white lounge chairs this past summer, a perfect specimen of masculinity, or so she had then believed. Now she understood. How good of God for protecting her from whatever harm could have come her way because of Kirk. Still, seeing Kirk for who he was didn't quell the deep sadness that filled her.

Her thoughts were interrupted by the telephone ring.

"Tena, are you all right? The voice coming through the receiver was full of anxious concern. "I tried to reach you at your office, but they told me that you had left for the day."

"Mike said to take some time, Oh, God, Johnny, something terrible…"

"I know. Have you been watching tv?"

"No, I've been home an hour or so, trying to think. I'm drained."

"I'm sure."

"There's a full blown story in the paper. I'm surprised that I haven't heard from my mother yet."

"You will. It's all over the news; on television too – the murder, Kirk, the whole story. What an awful, ungodly, rotten mess. You know I thought my newly acquired cousin was no good, but he sure didn't deserve this."

"None of them did," Tena responded feebly.

"I'm leaving the construction site in about a half an hour and I'm coming right over – don't say no; I'm coming."

"I wasn't going to say anything like that at all. I'll be more than glad to see you. I really don't want to be alone. But will it be okay if you leave?"

"Bud's going to take over. It will be okay."

"What I mean is that I have decided that I want to go up to North Creek later, and Johnny, there's something else here at the apartment that I want to show you. It's something very important that you should see."

"What are you saying? What's going on, Tena? Do you want to go up north tonight?"

"No, but maybe tomorrow, I think. And, of course, I'll want to go to Kirk's funeral."

"What are you telling me?"

"I just want to go, all right?"

"Is there something about you and Kirk that I should know?"

"I can't talk about this on the phone, Johnny. Not now. And no, Johnny, there is not one thing about Kirk and me that you don't already know. I wish that you would go to the funeral with me, but if you don't see your way clear to going up…"

"No, I'm fine with it," Johnny cut in. "I don't know what I'm saying. I guess this murder has got us both on edge. I'll drive you up there, and I'll make the necessary arrangements. I don't want you going alone."

"Okay," Tena whispered back. She was exhausted and her headache wasn't any better.

"I'll board the dogs with Doc Bender for the night and get a room over at Strolheim's Motel. As soon as I get myself situated, I'll be over to your place. I'll be there as soon as I can, and Tena..." he hesitated.

"What?"

"I want you to know. I guess you know..."

"I know, and double for me," Tena whispered into the receiver.

She hung up and shortly thereafter the front doorbell rang. Opening the door cautiously with the chain still on, she peeked around the side. To her astonishment, George MacArthur stood in the hallway. "May I come in for a few minutes?" he asked.

"Of course," Tena mumbled, sliding the lock off.

As George stepped into the living room, Tena apologized, "Forgive my appearance," and then she added, "I'm extremely sorry, George, especially for Lillian. Would you like to sit down, or have a cup of coffee? I can make some for us."

"No thanks," George replied. "I'll only take a few minutes of your time. I just flew in from LA. I left California as soon as I could because of this terrible news with Kirk. My Lil is devastated." His voice cracked.

"I can imagine," Tena replied gently while noticing his fatigued, rumpled demeanor.

George cleared his throat. "I was in touch with my wife right after my plane landed, and she told me that you had called."

"Yes, I did. I received your check, and of course I wanted to discuss it with you, George."

"I figured that you would. Anyway, the airport is just a few miles from here so I thought that I'd take a chance and stop by. What with how things are, I doubt that we'd have a chance to talk privately for some time, and there are things that need saying."

Tena could see that George was groping for his words. She found herself feeling sorry for him. "It's perfectly all right, George. I'm glad you stopped."

George continued nervously, "I should have personally given you the money and an explanation weeks ago. I should have been a man about all of this from the get-go." He stood up and walked toward the collage of family photographs hanging on the wall, examining each of them as he spoke. "Lillian has no idea that I sent it to you. Naturally, I plan to tell her, but now, as things stand, I believe it's best that she doesn't know about our meeting or the money." His words, he knew, were as mixed up as his thoughts, but no matter, he had to get this over with. He stood with his back to Tena, staring at her mother and Otto's portrait.

Tena slumped into a nearby chair feeling that she should say something consoling. "Please have a seat, George. I feel very bad about Kirk, he was..." her voice faltered briefly, and then she said thoughtfully, "a nice guy. I'm planning to come up for the funeral and give Lillian my condolences in person."

Turning toward her, George faced her head-on. "Let's be honest, Tena, Kirk couldn't control himself. I know it's not good to speak ill of the dead, but this is the hour...my hour... for honesty. Kirk had his good points, but he was weak."

Tena stared at him through swollen eyes. She was dumbfounded by his comment. "George, there was a lot of good in Kirk."

George offered up a slightly forced choked laugh. "I know what you're thinking. You're thinking that I'm a poor excuse for an uncle, a low life rat to think this way about a young man who was also my business partner. I should not speak ill of the dead, Tena, but I'm through lying to myself. It's a long flight in from L.A., and I had time to make a few decisions while I was up there."

"No one deserves to die that way, George."

The older man gripped the arms of the chair he had just sat in. He stared at the beige, shag carpet. "Of course not, and I never wished Kirk anything but the best. I really wanted to give him the benefit of the doubt. In the beginning, when he first came to us, I thought that life was going to be good for him in North Creek, and his being there would be good for my wife and me. For a while everything seemed to be going fine. The Pine Cone business picked up, and Lil was just delighted to have a member of her family around her, but I always knew that boy's wandering eyes would be his downfall. Unfortunately, Kirk had a sickness. He just couldn't leave women alone."

Tena was growing increasingly uncomfortable. "I really don't think that we should be having this conversation," she said gently.

George didn't want to hear her. "I'm glad that you weren't anymore involved with him than you were, and that you weren't caught in the crossfire the other night."

Tena remembered her moonlight warning and shuddered.

George continued, "You have no idea how much I have thanked the Lord about that. I would never have been able to forgive myself had you been hurt. You see, I know that you came to North Creek seeking answers about Ben. Your questions should have been answered years ago. We wouldn't have had to be here suffering through this painful conversation today."

Tena sighed wearily, "I still plan to come up for the funeral," she said.

"I thought you would," George remarked quietly.

"So George, why are you here? I know that you don't want me to mention the $25,000 to Lillian."

George nodded his affirmation. "I thank you for not saying anything to her on the phone. He glanced again at the photographs on the wall. "I never met your mother, but I knew your father well. He was a fine man, Tena, a good, honest gentleman in the truest sense of the word. You obviously are much like him."

Tena felt a tightening in her chest.

George said, "That money repays a loan that your father made to me many years ago."

"George, I appreciate…"

He rose from his chair and began pacing the room. "Let me finish. Everyone thinks that Lil came from a fine old Virginia family with a lot of money, but the truth is that her father ran off when she, her sister, and her brother were not much more than babies. He was an abusive drunk who beat her mother and her kid brother, James. He knocked him so hard once that he caused the boy to lose sight in his right eye. Lil's mother had her husband arrested that time, and when he got out of jail he took off to Canada. I'm sure Lillian's mother was grateful that he did."

Tena envisioned the sophisticated Lillian. It also occurred to her that the violent man George spoke of was Johnny's grandfather.

George seated himself again. "When Lillian was sixteen she quit school and went to work as a live-in domestic for a wealthy woman in Richmond. It was there that she learned to mimic the ways of a refined southern lady, while her own poor mother took in rich folk's washing and ironing to feed the family."

George hesitated for a moment. It was obvious that recounting his wife's past was painful. "I know there is no shame in an honest day's work, but you couldn't possibly understand how it is with someone like my wife. When Lillian came north she gave everyone the impression that she was a woman of extensive, fine breeding, and that it was she who had backed our investment in the inn. She couldn't live with the notion that her neighbors would think any different. She wouldn't want anyone to know about her past life. So you see, what else could I do? You have to understand. My beautiful Lillian worked dog hard cultivating herself, and after a time she had reinvented her entire life. She was so good at making everyone else believe her story that eventually she came to believe in the fairytale herself."

Tena laid her hand on George's arm. She could see that he was filled with anguish. "Why don't you let me make us some coffee?" she offered again.

"No, but I do thank you."

"I think that what you're trying to tell me is that my father had money in the Pine Cone Inn?"

"Yes, he financed a portion of the initial money, and the other part came from a government loan."

"And this money came from an inheritance. Right?"

"You know about that?"

Tena nodded. "I did some detective work on my own when I was in Warrensburg. I looked things up at the county courthouse, and I know that my father should have come into some money."

"Your research was on track. Back sometime after the war, Ben and his brother inherited a good sum of money, and your father later insisted that I take nearly every cent of his share as a loan to help me out with the purchase of the Pine Cone.

"I argued with him about it, but he wouldn't have it any other way. He wanted to save the old place from the wrecking ball, which was what Henderson's group had planned for it. Ben told me that the property had been sold by your granddad as part of the big land package deal. Your father went on about how his dad had been deceived during the negotiations for the sale of his property, and all he kept saying was that he had to save the inn. Your Uncle Bob was long gone out west; I think he had taken his share of the inheritance and reinvested it out there. All I know is that Ben said not to count on any help from Bob.

"In the beginning, I thought I could handle the expense of running the inn on my own, and I felt that I could turn a good profit in no time at all. But, before I put in my bid, I hired a builder friend of mine to inspect the property, and he had made it clear that in order to bring it around I would need a lot more money than I had in hand. The centuries had taken a toll, besides which the day-to-day operation of the place was let go by the man who was managing it for Hank when he got so sick. So, I scratched my IOU on a piece of paper one night, and your dad and I both signed it, but Ben told me to "get lost" when I tried to give him a copy, and I deposited your father's money the following week. Most of it went into repairs that Lil and I couldn't do ourselves, and after a year or so the old place was up and running. Next thing you know, your father was dead, and my wife and I just let our debt die with him. I'm sorry for that."

"But, I don't understand something, George. Wasn't my father married to my mother when he got his inheritance?"

"Yes, I believe that he was, but I doubt that he ever told her about the loan. I know that your mother never contacted me about it. If anything had come up about it and your mother had questioned him, I'm sure that he would have told her. I really have no answers for you about that. I do know that whatever he did, he had your future in mind. In retrospect, it must have been a tough call for him giving the money over to our investment. I know these sacrifices blanketed you and your mother for a long time, and this knowledge shames me. But, you have to believe that your father was doing what he felt was the only thing that he could do. Don't you think badly of him, and tell your mother the same. The sin of all that has happened is entirely on my back."

"My mother would never have asked," Tena commented dully.

"Your father moved away from North Creek, but he never lost his connection to the town. How could he when he owned a part of it, and his roots went down miles deep into Adirondack soil."

Tena observed George thoughtfully, and then, seeking confirmation for something she believed she already had the answer to, asked, "What about Johnny? Why do I have this check in my hands for $25,000 and not half of that amount?"

George held her gaze. "Because John Van Ness is not Ben Waldron's son, not a brother to you, but I think that you already know that, don't you?"

"Yes, we've both known for a while."

"That's good; now you can start your relationship on a good footing." He stood and stepped toward the door. "Look, I've got to get going. I've said my piece. The money is rightfully yours, Tena. Do what you want with it."

"I won't cash the check until you tell me that you've discussed all of this with your wife. I wouldn't feel right otherwise."

George smiled wanly. "I appreciate that, but there is something else."

"What?"

"I've decided to include your name on the deed to the Pine Cone, so I'll be making my confession to Lil as soon as the right moment shows itself to include that bit of news too. You'll also be receiving a call from our attorney about all of this shortly."

"George..."

"No, now listen, if I had done what was right all those years ago, well, let's just say that you have a lot of interest that I figure you're entitled to in addition to that $25,000. Right now, I don't know how to make all that up to you, but I plan to come up with something. Your name on the deed is a down payment."

Tena walked George to the door. "What can I say to you?" she asked gently.

"You don't have to say a thing, young lady. I was ashamed for years of how I let Ben down by turning my back on a responsibility. Now, maybe I can start to find my self-respect once again, and then there might be a chance for me when I meet my buddy up there. Hopefully, he'll grab hold of my hand and pull me through the pearly gates."

Tena fought to keep the tears from welling up in her eyes. She pitied George. She said, "I do forgive you. I feel that you have suffered enough over this."

"I appreciate your saying that," George whispered.

"I still have a million questions about my father. I'd still like to know more about him; things he liked to do, and places he went to when he was a boy. I'd like it if you and I could talk again sometime. I didn't come looking for money, George. I came to learn who my father was."

George nodded and reached toward her. "Sometime later when all this terrible grief has cleared away..." he said his voice trailing off. He released her hand and turned away, walking through the doorway and down the hallway toward the elevator.

Tena watched as the elevator doors parted and shut. She closed her apartment door.

Now she began to understand her father's sorrow. He had obviously felt compelled to make a decision that had placed the value of the land of his forbearers above the financial well being of her and her mother. When he saw the terrible burden that he had placed upon the shoulders of the woman he loved, he couldn't face the consequences of his actions. He had sought consolation in a bitter place. It was apparent that this deceptive choice brought him to an untimely death. It was also clear that the dark cell in which he died wasn't a concrete room enclosed by bars, but his own stifled heart.

Tena decided to make a pot of coffee after all. Johnny would be there soon, and with him would be the opportunity for beginning a whole new life.

She knew weeks ago that she cared for Johnny deeply. She believed that her feelings were those of love, but she was in no hurry. Her mother often said that it would take time for the Lord's plan to flower. Tena had begun to appreciate her mother's wisdom.

She also understood that the possibilities of this newly born realization of a new love filling her soul with growing happiness wasn't going to be her entire being. She had learned to listen to God's gift of direction through many sources: her family, friends, ancestors, but most of all through her inner voice. She had searched for her father, and Ben Waldron had definitely touched her, but she had been blessed with so much more along the way. She could see that much contributes to the life that human beings make for themselves on this earth.

Dreams sometimes pave the way to action, but the life lived is the total choice of the complete self. The solid fact was that she, Tena Waldron, could stand alone, one very confident person, shining within her own grace.

Epilogue

It took Lillian MacArthur over a year to recover from the terrible shock of her nephew Kirk's death, and another year before she openly acknowledged John Van Ness as the son of her deceased brother, James. During that time the Pine Cone's doors remained closed to the public.

It was difficult for Lillian to face the community after Kirk's murder, but her fears eventually were put to rest as friends and neighbors rallied to the support of the dignified Southern woman who had always treated her Northern neighbors with respect and genuine regard.

She and George reopened the Pine Cone Inn in the spring of 1978, once again with a silent partner, Ben Waldron's daughter, Tena. At George's insistence the inn was renamed, *Garret's Legacy* and the new enterprise flourished with tremendous success during the following four years.

When George died in 1982, Lillian's husband's dream was sold to Mr. And Mrs. Adrian Van Horn of New York City. Before his death George had compensated Kirk's parents for his investment in the inn.

The Van Horns, avid antique collectors, were delighted with their unique piece of Americana. They bought the old property with most of the original furnishings, however, all of the seventeenth century Dutch Majolica and silver pieces were immediately conveyed to Tena.

Tena suspected that at least one piece, a large blue and white bowl, belonged to a distant ancestor, Tennake Waldron, who had come as a bride from Holland over three hundred years before, and for whom Tena was named by her father, Ben Waldron. Some years later it was determined that the caudle cup with the "W" engraved upon it had been manufactured by an eighteenth century New York City silversmith. The original owner of the cup has never been established.

The day after the papers for the sale of the inn were signed, Lillian MacArthur left the state of New York for good, returning home to her beloved Virginia, where she now lives with her sister in an upscale retirement community just outside of Richmond.

Tena and Johnny were married in 1979. Three years later they were blessed with twin boys, Brian and Mark. The family lives, along with their two Labrador dogs, on fifteen acres in a home that Johnny built near the perimeter of Niskayuna, New York. There is a carved, wooden sign tacked to a tree as you enter their driveway. It reads, *"Van Ness's Heaven"*

Their family continues to dine on pot roast every Thursday at Bertha and Otto's little, white frame house.

As a wedding gift, Bertha presented her youngest daughter and new son-in-law with a piece of her exquisitely fashioned needlepoint. The following words are lovingly crafted;

"When things go wrong, as they sometimes will,

When the road you're trudging seems all uphill,

When the funds are low and the debts are high

And you want to smile, but you have to sigh,

When care is pressing you down a bit,

Rest! If you must—but never quit."

Author unknown

Tena and Johnny visited the three lovely ladies at Garnet Manor often during the years. Several times Bertha joined them.

Tess Waldron outlived both of her friends, Olive and Florence, passing away at the grand old age of 102. After Tess's funeral, Tena told her mother that she believed it was an angel who led her to North Creek, an angel she had encountered in the cemetery, and an angel who spoke to her through the light of a northern moon.

End

Resolved Waldron's signature

(b. 10 May 1610;   d. 1690)

Acknowledgements

First, and most importantly, I thank my husband, Andrew, for his multiple reads, editorial suggestions, creative cover photography, and unending "patience".

I acknowledge and thank Mrs. Doris Patton, the Johnsburg New York Town Historian, for all of her unwavering willingness to help with family records as well as locating several ancestral gravesites within the Union Cemetery at North Creek.

Thanking too, Mr. Dennis C. Ambrose of Black River, New York, for sharing his genealogical finds.

I'd like to remember and thank James Richards for writing his detailed, historical account, <u>1765 – JUDGE JOHN RICHARDS – 1865: HISTORIC ADIRONDACK SURVEYOR</u>. Thanks too, Jim, for your mention of so many long departed North Country souls.

I would also like to acknowledge and thank Andrew Mays for once again "getting the story concept" resulting in a terrific cover design.

Again, my thanks to Helen K. Hosier for continued support.

And finally, my love as well as thanks to dear friends, Martine and Bill Stapleton, for being there through all.

Ordering Information

Signed copies of THE DIARY OF A NORTHERN MOON as well as the author's first novel, MANHATTAN SEEDS OF THE BIG APPLE, are available for purchase by contacting New Beginnings by Katcas, email: sales@katcas.com Signed Copies may also be ordered via telephone by calling

New Beginnings by Katcas, Poestenkill, New York, Toll Free 877-349-2986.

Books can be ordered through the publisher, AuthorHouse Book Orders: Toll Free – 888-280-7715 or www.authorhouse.com

Both titles are also available through, www.amazon.com or www.barnesandnoble.com as well as your favorite book retailer.

About the Author....

Gloria Waldron Hukle is an 11th generation Waldron and a native of New York State. She and her husband, Andrew, reside in Averill Park, New York. For information on event schedules and reviews, please visit
www.gloriawaldronhukle.name